The Freedom to Stay

As the habitable areas of the Earth shrink under climate change, and as many governments around the world adopt measures to deport migrants and refugees, it is time to reexamine our traditional notion of freedom.

In the western tradition, freedom is generally understood in relation to space: it is the freedom of movement and the freedom not to be obstructed in one's movement by the state or anyone else. In *The Freedom to Stay*, von Redecker puts forward the radical argument that we should think of freedom in temporal rather than spatial terms. This means thinking of freedom as the capacity to endure in time and to have the time to be and do as one wishes. This reorientation aligns human liberty with ecological concerns.

Combining vivid personal narrative with rigorous philosophical argument, von Redecker shows that freedom is best realized when understood as fulfilled time. The political act of staying ties freedom to material conditions. It requires that habitable space be provided for everyone, including all nonhuman forms of life around us. Staying also reconnects freedom with desire. It channels the urge to live in all creatures, celebrates the ensuing abundance, and honors the specifically human aspiration for free and fulfilled time.

The Freedom to Stay

For the Six O'Clock Society

The Freedom to Stay

Eva von Redecker

Translated by Lucy Duggan

polity

The translation of this book was supported by a grant from the Goethe-Institut.

GOETHE
INSTITUT

Polity Press
65 Bridge Street
Cambridge CB2 1UR, UK

Polity Press
111 River Street
Hoboken, NJ 07030, USA

ISBN-13: 978-1-5095-7429-2
ISBN-13: 978-1-5095-7430-8(pb)

A catalogue record for this book is available from the British Library.

Library of Congress Control Number: 2026936562

Typeset in 11 on 13 pt Sabon by
Cheshire Typesetting Ltd, Cuddington, Cheshire
Printed and bound in Great Britain by Ashford Colour Ltd

For further information on Polity, visit our website:
politybooks.com

Contents

Introduction: The Arrival of the Swallows

The freedom to stay

Do you know how it feels when the swallows come back? I don't know anyone who has lived near barns or farm buildings and doesn't attach special meaning to that moment. It is a festive day, almost like Christmas or May Day. The most conventional farmer, with umpteen thousand chickens vegetating in his poultry sheds as they wait to be slaughtered, still props open the barn windows so that the swallows can easily fly in and out. The gardeners in the next village have made clay bowls so that the nests under the tin roof don't get too hot. Even lesbians curse their cats. In the midst of the daily grind of the dawning Anthropocene, swallows have remained holy.

But the date isn't marked in advance in the calendar, and we don't organize the festival ourselves. We don't do anything at all, other than tell each other about it. "The swallows have come back here – have you seen any at your place?" Part of the magic is the fact that the swallows don't even fully come back to us. Unlike other songbirds, they hardly ever land on the earth. It is only for building their nests that they collect small balls of mud from the ground; they bring a bit of earth up high, so that they can live on it there. Hunting and drinking take place in the air. Swallows remain in their element. And our world opens out a little when we see these seemingly weightless bodies looping the loop over our roofs. They're not ours – but still they come to us.

During the first wave of the pandemic, I was supposed to travel to the United States to give some talks. Invitations that I was originally very happy about. But when it became clear that I wouldn't be able to travel, I was strangely indifferent. In fact, I was relieved. It suddenly seemed like a stroke of luck, as if a crime had narrowly been prevented. What had I been thinking – to imagine getting on a plane these days and pumping CO_2 into the atmosphere? With a manuscript on my lap for a talk about authoritarianism but trapped in my old habits? But the sense of freedom on that day did not come from an unburdened conscience. It's not as if I had done something right. It was just an astonishing pleasure to feel that everything was open – no plans, no deadlines today – and then came a particularly auspicious gift. On that very day, the swallows came back. And I was there.

Freedom of movement

"The freedom to stay" is what I tried calling it. Being free not to go anywhere. That is obviously paradoxical. Why call it freedom when a flight is canceled? Especially since I didn't even have to accept those invitations in the first place. And now that the trip was planned, I was being prevented from taking it – I hadn't chosen that. Being forced to stay put cannot be called freedom. Even aside from my concrete situation, the idea of remaining in one place goes against freedom's connotations.

After all, in the western tradition, "freedom" is inseparable from freedom of movement. Thomas Hobbes, who founded modern political philosophy with his *Leviathan* in the mid-seventeenth century, declared: "LIBERTY, or FREEDOME, signifieth (properly) the absence of Opposition; (by Opposition, I mean externall Impediments of motion;)."[1] One hundred years later, the British jurist William Blackstone wrote that individual freedom consisted of "locomotion" – the ability to move.[2] The mechanical notion of freedom as unhindered movement may seem rather simplistic, but it also underpins more complex versions of the concept. If freedom is derived from the autonomous will, it is measured by the scope for decision making within which that will can operate. Liberal freedom always relies on a spatial imaginary, to the point that it is practically codified as a geometric shape. Legally delineated spheres within which we should not be limited by anything apart from the fact that others have the same rights as we do – this is what the institutional framework of liberal freedom secures. But already before freedom was defined in revolutionary terms as a human right, it could be experienced as a change of place: the free people are those who leave Egypt for the Promised Land. A free city is one where *corvée* has been abolished, and free states are the Northern States where slavery is banned.

Freedom of movement was also one of the key points of leverage heralding the end of undemocratic state socialism. And no doubt one of the gravest injustices of the present day consists in the way in which national borders have been fortified to make global inequality ever more entrenched at the cost of tens of thousands of human lives. The sense of open horizons when we see birds migrating is still something that humans have not succeeded in realizing for ourselves. My German passport allows me to travel to 191 countries without a visa. A citizen of Zimbabwe, where many swallows spend the other half of the year, is barely allowed to travel to a third of those – the northern ones least of all.

Given that freedom is so closely associated with freedom of movement, it is no surprise that many experienced the pandemic travel restrictions as a drastic loss of freedom – and not just when they confined people to cramped or violent households. Freedom is freedom of movement. If we look at freedom like this and see it as a scale, staying in one place is at zero.

Shattered freedom

I would probably have dismissed the notion of "the freedom to stay" as one of the idiosyncrasies of a homebody who would rather stick to her desk and her vegetable garden, if it hadn't been echoed by some of the fundamental political demands of the present day. In Germany, protesters against coal mining insist that "all villages stay"; defenders of the forests say, "Danni stays," "Moni stays," or "Fechi stays," using nicknames to refer to the places they are trying to preserve.[3] "We're all staying" is the rallying cry against gentrification and displacement from the city. Against every deportation of asylum seekers, there is the demand for a safe place to stay. The LGBT emancipation movements place a similar emphasis on the refusal to move: "We're here. We're queer. Get used to it." And when the conservation board fixes signs on farm buildings that are particularly swallow friendly, it is once again about making sure that the nests can stay, so that the non-monogamous pairs of birds can faithfully return to them.[4]

But the fact that people demand to be able to stay does not mean that staying is a freedom. Isn't it more about security? Or – at most – about "life"? Or perhaps simply protection of the environment, protection of minorities? And such protection, if you listen to public discourse, is currently under outright suspicion of destroying freedoms.

Over the last few years, there has in fact been no more effective maneuver, when it comes to undermining progressive demands, than the appeal to freedom. What was once the central value of the 1968 generation is now fuel for the campaigns of Meloni, Milei and Trump. I don't see that as a simple takeover. It is more like the uncovering of a fracture that has always run through the liberal notion of freedom, the fracture between despotism and restraint. Within the geometry of liberal freedom, modern individuals are not just posited as players. They are owners, if only of themselves. Thus, freedom promises, on the one hand, that we can all rule unimpeded over particular sectors of the world. On the other hand, this freedom obliges us not to encroach on the claims of other people. Thus, the lack of moderation is moderated. Even in the best case, there remains an obvious tension between these two sides. If things don't go well, they become unhinged. In almost every heated public debate – whether it's about protecting people from infection, or about discrimination, migration, sustainability – the drama is repeated: each side waves around one piece of the shattered notion of freedom, the claim to ownership versus the boundaries of consideration for others. It is as if we were beating each other over the head with these broken pieces. And it seems fair to say that the piece with "possessiveness" written on it proves to be the more effective weapon.

The campaigns to be able to stay – against deportation and demolition – could be described as spearheading the side of restraint. The demand that something or someone should stay calls for new boundaries here and now, as lines of defense – boundaries that stand in the way of possessive entitlement. This stance could hardly be embodied more clearly right now than by the activists of the environmental group Last Generation who glue their bare hands to the tarmac. In a way, they turn themselves into a barrier. Facing them, shaking their heads, are people whose everyday lives are already so full of obstacles that they don't know how to endure a further complication. And some of them are obsessed with claiming ownership over mobility, so they jump out of their cars with raised fists. The outdated, hollow claim to power over others, which I describe as phantom possession, is all the more likely to flip into violence in an instant.

But is that really it? Are the additional obstacles the aim of the protests? Or are they not in fact a distorted version of a more far-reaching demand, translating it into the pictures we're used to? What if it's not primarily about redrawing the boundaries, but about a different notion of how we relate to each other in the first place? The position of those who stubbornly remain on runways or "zones to be defended" could also be interpreted differently. Not as an extreme point in a familiar space, but as the emergence of something quite new. However, this would not be a space at all, but a different time. Because the idea of staying departs from the spatial imaginary of liberal freedom and refers instead to the possibilities of the future. On the spatial axis, staying might not represent any kind of freedom. But in the dimension of time, it might well be freedom's fullest expression.

Staying here, and staying free. The pandemic restrictions can already be justified better if they are detached from immediate freedom of movement. They were about the freedom to be more carefree again with other people at some point. Staying at home now so as to be able to travel more easily in the future: to think like this, we have to be able to see freedom in temporal terms. No longer flying now so that we'll be able to breathe later. But is that actually possible? Can we imagine freedom in temporal terms?

Future freedom

In its remarkable ruling of March 24, 2021, the German constitutional court decided that it was unlawful to distribute climate protection measures very unequally across time. If we don't do anything, today's young people will be forced into all the more drastic restrictions a few decades from now. That would mean that we are using our freedom right now at their expense. The court itself describes this temporal perspective as "the intertemporal guarantee of freedom," thus enabling itself to put forward an unusual – even revolutionary – argument. The justification for the ruling dispenses with the usual dependence on the present, which would mean that freedom could only be claimed by those who were actually here. This orientation toward the future is only possible because the federal government itself has signed the Paris Agreement and thus pledged to make its contribution to limiting global warming to 1.5 degrees. This prevents the claims which will be raised in the future from becoming endless and overwhelming. At this point, it is clearly possible to see which emissions can still be given off. If the budget is used up, logically nothing will be left. Likewise, the delayed development of alternative forms of transport affects the future. More traditional mobility now means less mobility later.

Without meaning to underplay the significance of this legal decision, it is still important not to read too much into it. The notion of freedom with which the decision operates is still that of scope for movement versus barriers. In fact, the freedom which is supposed to be fairly distributed consists of the ownership of fuel. Protecting the environment is seen as absolutely necessary but is approached as a block to freedom. The idea that freedom could be found in the riches of a living, biodiverse world or in the collective power derived from reinventing our form of life: that doesn't come into it.

For good reasons, the court is not responsible for fully revising the constitutional notion of freedom, and the concept of intertemporality is already very daring. But truly seeing freedom in temporal terms would encompass much more than just taking the same freedom to travel and saving it for the future. It could mean measuring freedom itself according to the amount of available, livable time. Not: how much space can I take up? But: how much time is allotted to me? Now, later, and in the long run? From freedom across time, we would arrive at freedom in time – being granted an abundance of time. The freedom to stay can bring these aspects together. Do we want to give this freedom to those who live around us and in the future?

It is not easy to shift our thinking so that we imagine freedom itself as time. It is not simply a thought experiment; it has implications for all our impulses and interests. "Full speed ahead!" – we all know that feeling. But what do we feel when we have the freedom to stay? It is like being able to exhale. The freedom to stay implies freedom from fear. "I'll tell you what freedom is to me. No fear," in the words of Nina Simone.[5] If we do not have to be so afraid or put up so many barriers, we are more capable of action, and only then can we act in our own unique ways – we can "be different without fear," as Theodor Adorno puts it in *Minima Moralia*.[6] So it means truly being able to breathe, and it means an expansive field of view, with many more starting points.

The freedom to stay grants us the intense, unhoped-for sensation of being able to live without being under threat.

This sensation is thanks to the certainty that the place where we are is truly not a prison. This means that where the freedom to stay starts, unfreedom really ends. In contrast with this, mere freedom of movement has a catch: it leaves unfreedom unaffected. It just means that we are elsewhere. In an extreme case, we even need continuing social injustices as a contrast, to keep on reminding ourselves that we ourselves are free. That downgrades the freedom we have achieved – the place where we can breathe a different air – turning it into a merely comparative quantity. At least it's better than before. Or even: at least it's not exactly the same as before. This lets us comfortably conceal the question of whether that's all. Whether we have even reached the right place. The freedom to stay does not depend on any such comparison. The realization that we are not in prison would continue to stand, even if there were no real prisons anywhere. It is not a comparison – "in prison it would be worse than it is at home" – but an experience. I can remain here, and remain free. And this experience is under much greater threat and is disappearing much more quickly than the freedom to travel, much as the latter may be regulated by political decisions.

If we have a place to stay and be free, we are very lucky. It is a gift – not in the sense of a talent but in the sense of good fortune. The struggles I have mentioned for the right to stay are devoted to the task of making this basic foundation available to everyone. The aim is to secure a future with lasting freedom for everyone. That is the point of fighting for open borders: so that those whose freedom to stay is precarious where they are are fully entitled to arrive, thrive and stay somewhere else. In protests against oppression and in workers' struggles, free access to time is at stake; conservationists and the health service want to secure future time for life and living things. Nevertheless, as a concept, the freedom to stay does not in itself already make a categorical decision. So you could also argue that children should stay at school in a pandemic, that a tradition should remain alive or that a coal mine should remain active, if you could prove that these things realized freedom across time.

The vanishing world

Our usual concept of freedom is unfit for the Anthropocene. It reacts sensitively if anyone comes close to denting our ability to move around in petrol-burning metal boxes. But the question of whether there will still be birds in the future leaves it completely unmoved. Where landscapes have been made uninhabitable by war and natural disasters, permission to travel is an emergency measure, more like forced migration than a freedom. The flight of the swallows should also not be idealized excessively as a freedom: the birds leave because in the cold, wet season in the north there is not much to eat. Just as the freedom to stay assumes that we would be allowed to leave, freedom of movement is only freedom if staying would also be possible. And that – the possibility of staying – is the more demanding part. It requires that we preserve a habitable world.

Within my lifetime, if I get to live it in full, large parts of the surface of the earth that are currently settled will become uninhabitable. The climate question is on most people's minds by now. As we have seen, it has reached the highest court in Germany. But just like the Paris Agreement, which has remained unimplemented and which in any case only takes account of emissions, this consciousness of the climate crisis has no effect. The amount of CO_2 emitted rises to new heights every year. We are still on course for a world where temperatures will be at least four degrees higher than in pre-industrial times. Rainforests, glaciers, and coral reefs will disappear, and the proportion of fertile land will be dramatically reduced. Even the latitudes that are spared – comparatively speaking – will frequently be afflicted by extreme weather events and floods, which will disturb deposits of toxic or radioactive waste, destroy infrastructure, and make basic necessities such as clean water scarce. In a world like that, is anyone going to be able to breathe?

But something about these evocations of the future seems dishonest. As if we were searching desperately for a tool that would manage to push past the pain barrier. I am more interested in tools that dispel numbness. The apocalypse is already here. In summer, I look up at the sky anxiously, and the air is so empty that I'm sometimes glad to be bitten by a mosquito. There has to be something for the swallows to eat. Even at the height of our fears for the coming catastrophe, the present is in some way exonerated. As if this right now were intact life. For those who are currently well off – including me and probably most people reading this book – everything we are afraid of is already happening to somebody right now. Most of the time we even profit from it. And even the truly new effects of global warming won't come from the future but from previous actions.

I don't believe, in any case, that we have to convince anyone that a collapse is coming. On the contrary: the sense of a collapsing world is omnipresent. In this phenomenally rich society, in the middle of all this technology and competence, there are no longer any reserves anywhere. A few decades of privatization, increased efficiency, and financialization, and suddenly everything is falling apart. The system no longer has any slack built in for emergencies to give us time to ward off the worst. The energy that people manage to find in exceptional situations is already planned into the normal running of a neoliberal world, as a fixed quantity. And it is because everyone can sense the impending emergency that the reactions drift so far apart from each other. From the standpoint of futurelessness, phantom possession and the grasping ruthlessness of self-assertion certainly have their own rationality. If we are no longer going to be able to participate in future wealth, then we at least want to make the most of what we can get in the general inferno. No one's going to take my bit of destruction away from me!

We are not simply going to stay in the Holocene, that friendly epoch which followed the last ice age twelve thousand years ago and allowed a luxurious number of ecosystems to flourish in concert with each other. But for that very reason, absolutely everything depends on how much we can take with us into the Anthropocene, to make a home for ourselves there.

The missing swallows

In the same spring that I did not fly to the United States, a good friend phoned me. Elisabeth is a generation older than me and used to be my history teacher. Like me, she comes from a farm in Northern Germany and lives in a house with a barn beside it. She spoke in a strangely flat voice, as if from a world without echoes. "Eva," she said, "the swallows haven't come back here this year." Silence. "Now it's really over," she said, and it sounded less like a complaint than like someone reading the result of a measurement. "Now I don't expect anything anymore."

The Australian nature philosopher Glenn Albrecht created the word "Solastalgia" in 2005 to describe the trauma arising from the loss of the familiar ecological surroundings. Nostalgia, but in real time: a longing not for something from the past, but for things we had thought were an unalterable part of the present.[7] Combining the Latin "solacium," meaning comfort, with the Greek "algia," from "algos" (pain), it is not a word that trips off the tongue. "Pain from a lack of comfort": that's not a bad description of how people are affected by a dying world. But I can't help wondering about this neologism because so much is missing from it. It does not mention the world, which is the object of longing. Nor does it mention the reason for its loss. The planet is not just dying of its own accord. The swallows are starving because the insects are dying out. In long dry periods they can't build nests because they need puddles of water in order to collect little balls of mud. In many regions, songbirds are also actively hunted. Solastalgia does not name those responsible, nor even the causes. No hint of insecticides, industrial emissions of CO_2 or air rifles. And after all, homesickness is also different if you have been forced to leave, rather than moving voluntarily.

Maybe "Weltschmerz" would be a better category than solastalgia since it would at least emphasize that this is about an overall context and not about an individual location which we can still leave behind. The barn is still standing. But for Elisabeth, time has stopped. Not clock time – which would still keep ticking away in the wristwatch of a corpse – but time that is living and lived. The time in which years coincide with the arrival and departure of the swallows: it has been destroyed. The shock at the absence of the four familiar breeding pairs does not only relate to eight birds and their offspring but is a sign of the sixth mass extinction. The lack of comfort does not arise because nothing can help to get over this loss, but because it isn't just about this one loss. What would be an obsessive thought in a normal experience of trauma – the sense that things will keep on being like this – is, in this case, a scientifically proven reality.

Given this reality, the echo of "nostalgia" in "solastalgia" is also outrageous. You can almost hear the governments of wealthier nations coming up with programs to develop solastalgia cures for their wealthier citizens, and funding research into the factors creating resilience – and apart from that, people can always say that we ought to be able to get over such sentimentalities as the irreplaceable connection with a place. Modernity didn't promise solace, after all; it promised freedom.

But was it the whole freedom? Isn't something crucial missing? Doesn't our freedom depend on the continuing existence of the living world? In fact, isn't that exactly what defines it?

The joy of the swallows

In order to connect freedom with life, we have to think temporally. That in turn raises the question of what we understand by "time." The moment of staying seemed freeing to me because it unexpectedly gave me more time, as well as the realization that I was happy to spend it in the place where I live. But there was more. The birds were arriving. In a certain sense, the swallows are part of the place. But maybe that is the wrong perspective; maybe it is precisely the other way round, and a place is nothing more than that: the intersection of various temporal cycles. Not just the wall, but the rays of spring sunshine that touch it and the blossoming pear trees in front of it. All of that is time. Not my time, but time that accommodates me. The seasonal migratory cycles of the birds, the position of the sun at different times of day, crop cycles and growing seasons. And even the wall, formed from different time periods: red clay from the Ice Age stratum of the earth, the heat of wood burnt two hundred years ago, the work of hands cooperating with other hands. When we are not talking about the unique span of an individual lifetime but about nature, we can describe this time as cyclical. Not simply time, not an empty future, but tides, in abundance. And that is what it could mean to see freedom temporally: an abundance of time and tides. To allow real freedom, free time also has to mean time that is filled, or even fulfilled. Inwardly, we know that very well; it is the difference between boredom and experiences; between time that drags and time filled with things we can do and things we want to do. But what fills our time does not come from us. Living a full life also means living in a time of fullness.

Joy at the return of the swallows is older than the threat that now hangs over them. In the horror of the sixth mass extinction, swallows as a species are actually in a relatively good position. They are adaptable; they can change their flight routes. The familiar *Hirundo rustica* is currently only listed as "decreasing" and is not on the actual Red List. Weighing twenty grams, with a red spot on the throat and elegantly forked tail feathers, it is still a small miracle that any of these little creatures survive, even without the end of the world. The freedom to stay points to the unique possibility of being there for their arrival, not missing the moment of joy and relief. Ten thousand kilometers of wind and weather, and suddenly they're back, safe and well.

The joy at the arrival of the swallows is an echo of the time when we went hungry in the winter, shivering and longing for the season of plenty. The swallows were the messengers of the material abundance of the tides. But that does not fully explain the sense of joy. We don't necessarily need the swallows to tell us that it's getting warmer. The swallows allow us an extra moment to pause, a moment of fascination with this particular facet of life. Something about their joyful high-pitched concert is infectious. It speaks to us, even if we can't translate it. Michel de

Montaigne, who was writing philosophy more than four hundred years ago, even saw a certain freedom at work in the swallows. He attributed to them the ability to judge a certain place and approve of it. "Do the swallows that we see on the return of spring ferreting in all the corners of our houses search without judgment, and choose without discrimination, out of a thousand places, the one which is most suitable for them to dwell in?"[8]

Swallows are synanthropic. Unlike other wild animals, they would not be better off if we were simply not around. It is our old walls that they find homely, and it is the insects flourishing in our dung that they find tasty. We don't need to do anything more than that. Their conditions of life arise from ours. This relationship is an example for a successful circular economy, in which different elements enable each other to regenerate. The swallows share our time, but that doesn't mean we have less of it. And we can enjoy their presence without it costing us anything. The freedom found in interactions which easily perpetuate themselves is a theme running through the balanced ecosystems of our planet, which have evolved to find that balance over hundreds of thousands of years. Our notion of history, just like our current economic system, is designed as if that background were simply a given. But abundance is actually a fragile undertaking. It exists when the tides are attuned to each other; it exists in the seemingly effortless way that the swallows live with us, which by itself is not enough to feed us. Absolutely all future freedom – even the freedom simply to leave – depends on how many of our supply cycles we manage to preserve through similarly regenerative relationships. The claim to the full freedom to stay brings this question to the fore. Can I stay here and stay free? Can we live on this planet without being in a constant state of terror, working laboriously against its catastrophes; can we stay here in such a way that we also stay free, enjoying an abundance of time, able to look up at a sky in which swallows are dancing?

Perhaps the joy of the swallows' arrival is not our joy at all, but theirs. Perhaps the jubilation of the swallows is transferred to us. They sing of their happiness at having found a place after their difficult journey – a place to stay for now. We share their joy and enjoy our own freedom.

1
An Abundance of Time

Alone on Mars

"Freedom means being alone on Mars." The twelve-year-old son of some friends of mine from Prague made this announcement at our dinner table, and I've been thinking about it ever since. He wanted to know what philosophers did. I said that we thought about concepts. That is, about the meaning of the words we use to refer to very fundamental things, which also often happen to be invisible. Freedom, for example. He hardly needed any time to think about it. Freedom was being alone on Mars. Astonished, I pressed for details: how would he make sure he didn't get bored? His parents wondered – rather anxiously – whether he'd miss them. But clearly, for my young colleague, all this was beside the point. Freedom means being alone because then it's really impossible for anyone to interfere. It means being left in peace, doing what you like.

It is not as if I don't have any sympathy for this point of view. Particularly coming from a middle child. I, too, find myself constantly longing for a solitary place to think and write. Mars does not attract me, but isolation certainly does. Does that mean that we – as gregarious earthlings, for better or for worse – can at best experience only something faintly approaching the greater freedom of Martians?

If being alone means freedom, wouldn't that actually mean that the moment of death is the greatest liberation? We may not go to Mars when we die, but at least we escape society. The catch, of course, is that we also stop existing. We are no longer there at all, and thus we can't do anything with our freedom. Perhaps that would have been a better rhetorical strategy: Alone on Mars, you wouldn't survive at all. As soon as you arrived, you'd be dead on the spot. No more freedom then. And even with a space suit, an oxygen mask, and plenty of supplies of astronaut food, the intensity of the radiation would first make you seasick and then give you cancer. That would be a particularly ruthless maneuver in the typical litany of adults: don't do it, it's dangerous. It probably wouldn't have impressed him much. He would have looked at me wearily and said that that was just a detail he'd left out; obviously we'd have to invent the technology and then, alone on Mars with the right equipment, he'd be free.

In a certain sense, this twelve-year-old had understood our semantics of freedom better than me and done what philosophers do: taken it to its logical conclusions. His suggestion combines an extreme freedom of movement – taking him straight to Mars – with the ultimate radius of the individual will: not limited by anything or anybody. Because that is exactly how the liberal tradition – the intellectual tradition spanning around four hundred years and pervading all constitutional states and our capitalist economic system – understands freedom. Except that the role of Mars is played by legislation, which creates spaces in which we can dream, undisturbed, of full control. At the beginning, in the work of Thomas Hobbes and

John Locke, who were writing in a seventeenth-century England battered by war, it was really about room to move for individual bodies. Those individual bodies ought to be protected from external violence by a ruling power capable of taking action, and they should be able to go about their business. Locke already saw that protection *against* such a ruling power could also be relevant. After the Atlantic revolutions, more nuanced forms of liberal freedom went on to delineate particular spheres within which the will should be unbounded. Specific rights guarantee us freedom of opinion, religion, association, and above all the freedom to hold property. The private realm is also a planet of its own: sexual relationships and family. Neither a stranger nor the state is supposed to be allowed to interfere there.

In the mid-nineteenth century, the English liberal John Stuart Mill wrote that everything that made his existence valuable depended on limitations on the actions of others. And already fifty years earlier, Immanuel Kant remarked resignedly that it was impossible, at least on earth, to get rid of other people: on a sphere, we always meet each other again, even if we try to walk away, and we have to adjust to this by staying within the areas allotted to us. To that extent, each individual will has limited freedom of movement: it cannot have too much effect on the arena of freedom allotted to other people. In return, however, it has free rein within its own arena. This compromise defines liberal freedom, and within it smolders a latent discontent. It is a reasonable compromise, but it rests on a certain irrationality: the tendency to tear down all boundaries in order to experience another, greater freedom in that very act. At least for a moment. Or else: the desire to get rid of everyone else, so that it would no longer be necessary to put any limits in place. We can retrospectively approve of reason, but still the simple formula, "I am free when I can do as I like," kindles a longing for an empty universe: I am free when I can finally do whatever the hell I want, without anyone being around who could be affected by it.

But on Mars, or within our demarcated rights to freedom, we wouldn't only get away from other people. We'd also get away from earth itself. In the exaggeration, something becomes clear which is already present in the common notion of freedom: indifference toward earthly life. It is because of that indifference that this is even possible: a smart speaker of our language is convinced, at least for a moment, that his freedom could be realized not only entirely alone but also entirely independently of the blue of our planet. This detachment helps to explain why "freedom" currently functions above all as the figurehead of devastation. If the earth is destroyed, then we can simply be free on Mars. All the death around us doesn't apply to us, not in our innermost core, not in our freedom. Or in fact it does apply to us, to the extent that we welcome it, in an eerie way. The less life there is around us, the more scope there is for the movement of the space-traveling individual will.

Why is it that we build our freedom according to the model of the least limited mobility? The most extreme freedom of movement is only attractive as long as we entirely disregard the dimension of time. Our inner image of freedom actually does look a lot like a giant rocky desert. Freedom is when nothing is in the way. But we view this emptiness with a will that vibrates with life, filled with vigor and impressions and intentions. That is, our view of it is shaped by an energy which often stumbles in the thicket of the everyday, and doesn't get to spread its wings: finally, the way is open! How often do we want to do something and find ourselves prevented by all the other things around us: colleagues, authorities, care commitments. The idea of having free rein attracts us, but only as a moment – a moment into which we can take everything that defines us and moves us. If we instead try to imagine this type of individual freedom over a long period of time, tedium takes over. Our drive for action, our attention span, and finally even our will to live melt away when nothing else is there but free rein. That's why we probably don't even imagine that. In any case, it is much more difficult to imagine time than space. After all, it is not a category of perception but of experience. I generally love films in which practically nothing happens, but even I wouldn't like to watch an hour and a half of Mars Rover footage. My young interlocutor would probably get bored after a two-minute TikTok video of nothing but red earth. Only very few people would really want to stay on Mars. It's just that we're not used to making the desire to stay the measure of freedom.

Something in us is fundamentally resistant to the perspective of staying. Perhaps it's the freedom-seeking drive to move. Or maybe it's a more deeply rooted dread of time. It is hard for us to keep ourselves and our freedom in mind across time. Because when we think this way, we are inevitably confronted with mortality: with the fact that after a while, every single one of us will be gone. Why should we put our faith in being able to stay for a certain length of time, when death will defeat us in the end? If I had told the space-travel pioneer that death would be waiting on Mars, he could have said: it's waiting on earth, too.

And from this stalemate position, my plea for a temporal perspective seems unlikely to succeed. If the search for freedom is always driven by a longing for the infinite, why should we force it into the limited, temporal span of a life, instead of seeking the maximum freedom of movement in a specific moment? Our time is limited. But space in the universe is infinite.

Xanthippe's company

Isn't time infinite too, though? Can't we stay in it, or with it, infinitely? That is the view of those who believe in life after death. Their understanding of freedom inevitably departs from freedom of choice in the moment. However, it also departs from the earth. For sailors, according to one belief, it is the swallows that bring the souls of the drowned to heaven. That is why they are a popular motif for tattoos. Among philosophers, the most influential argumentation for the immortality of the soul comes from Plato. In his dialogue *Phaedo*, he has Socrates defend this idea of eternity, which was actually an unusual one for antiquity – and for the historical Socrates. The circumstances could hardly be more dramatic since the scene of the dialogue is the prison cell where Socrates is awaiting his execution, which is set for that evening. Socrates has been convicted by an Athenian jury of corrupting the youth. He is determined not to avoid his sentence. This throws his loyal pupil, Plato, into a deep crisis. The fact that the democratic citizenry has decided to have its most outstanding member murdered destroys Plato's trust in politics – his *Republic* is evidence of this, with its obsessively planned city-state, controlled by philosophers. And the fact that Socrates' farewell is supposed to be final evidently means that for Plato, any life in this world has been robbed of meaning.

Thus, in *Phaedo*, at Socrates' deathbed, a philosophical reflection begins on the unbearableness of death. Or rather: it could have begun. Plato himself, according to the text, is indisposed. He has a fever and has stayed at home. Obviously, we don't actually know, but I imagine that he is so paralyzed by his fear of loss that he is incapable of facing the death of his idol. Perhaps he is also jealous that he cannot say goodbye in a more intimate setting because

Socrates has gathered a whole squad of friends, lovers, and pupils at his bedside. The thinker of the marketplace, he creates a public even at the last moment, one which in this case is also a polyamorous, gay, and sapiosexual cell.

At least one side of Plato, then, collapses at the prospect of saying goodbye. However, that is not the side that philosophizes in *Phaedo*. Or at least not explicitly. For the whole dialogue serves to play down horror and despair in the face of death. Yes, apparently a philosopher is even supposed to look forward to death since in his philosophizing all he has done is separate the soul from the body and practice dying. "Then when death comes to a man," Socrates proposes, "his mortal part, it seems, dies, but the immortal part goes away unharmed and undestroyed, withdrawing from death."[1] Measured against such freedom of movement, the amount of time we have spent on earth is unimportant. What counts is only that we use that time to gain a ticket to travel onward: according to Plato, not all souls manage to ensure that they live on; some are too attached to the physical realm to free themselves in death. Pleasure and pain are described by Socrates as nails that pin the soul to the body. If things go badly, the body remains the coffin of the soul. If they go well, however, it only imprisons the soul for a short time. Socrates assumes that the latter applies to him, and thus he forbids his friends to mourn him.

Certainly, Plato needs comfort. And there is something moving about seeing how Socrates, lively and contrary and generous as always, tries to prove to his friends through quite ludicrous arguments that there is no reason for lamentation. But there can be no comfort without first recognizing the truth of the pain. And that truth – in this hundred-page key text of western philosophy – is only formulated once, in the first pages. Xanthippe, Socrates' wife, is initially also present, visiting him in prison. Putting aside her own situation and fixing her attention on her spouse's inclinations, she cries in distress: "Oh Socrates, this is the last time now that your friends will speak to you or you to them."[2] It remains her only remark: as soon as she has said it, Socrates has her thrown out of the room.

We could interpret the pain articulated by Xanthippe as a wish for the freedom to stay: the wish that Socrates could be allowed to remain for a while among his friends. Perhaps there would even be a certain comfort for his friends in the idea that this wish to live on is for their sake, in particular. That would have been a start. Instead, Plato's Socrates-avatar introduces an overkill of freedom to stay, making the whole world unimportant in one fell swoop. What counts is the soul and its eternal life. Here the world is still the ancient cosmos, which is imagined as being eternal, in contrast with the Christian worldview that developed later. But what is important, what ought to be the aim of our actions, is suddenly no longer the earth. Nor is it the *polis* as a political community, as most Greeks would have argued. All that counts is the individual soul as a vehicle to evade death. It is supposed to gain access to another place, which Socrates calls the "real earth." Unlike ours, it is not "injured and corroded, as in the sea things are injured by the brine," not full of "endless mud and mire," but smooth, shining, and full of color.[3] It does not rely on water, but is nourished by ether. It does sound – I admit – slightly more attractive than Mars. But is it really more tempting than a finite life with the consolations of salt water and friends?

In my life, there are a few people who are very precious to me and at the same time quite frustrating: in our conversations, their stubbornness reminds me of Socrates in his typical dialogues. They resemble him in their tendency to insist on their own ignorance. Despite their enormous thirst for knowledge, they claim not to know anything.

But at the same time, they are incredibly skilled at picking apart any knowledge that is offered to them until it disintegrates back into ignorance. What remains is that wild desire for knowledge and my own entirely misguided hope of satisfying it. In other words, true love.

One of these people showed me something that came close to the Socratic ability to die. Jutta had multiple sclerosis and decided very early on and very fiercely that she would not seek treatment. I first visited her and her husband a few times with my parents, as an awkward teenager. Toward the end of my school days and the beginning of my studies, I visited more often, on my own. The key to the front door was always in the lock, on the outside. Her husband was at work during the day, after getting up before dawn to care for his wife and for the household. I just wandered in, like Socrates' pupils, wanting to talk. At the beginning, Jutta was still sitting in her wheelchair, and toward the end she lay in a bed in the living room, which opened directly off the hallway behind the front door.

These days, it is easy for me to reject Socrates' separation of body from soul, being well versed in feminist theory and other anti-dualistic approaches. After all, this separation is not only false, but fatal: already in Socrates' formulations, a rigid hierarchy emerges. "When the soul and the body are joined together," he says, "nature directs the one to serve and be ruled, and the other to rule and be master."[4] Together with St. Paul's hatred of the flesh, this triumph of the invisible over the visible went on to shape the hostility toward the body found throughout the Christian tradition. And as we will see, precisely this ruling power returns in the phantasm of sovereignty which declares the modern self to be the owner of itself. All of that – the ruling power, and eternal life – obviously has to be disputed. But something about the separation still applies. Or at least, that is what was burned into my memory during these visits. Every time, a transformation took place. At the start of the visit, I was always embarrassed, shocked by the visible deterioration. Dozing on the bed, her face gaunt, her fingers curled over the wool blanket, and her hair thinning, I was often worried that Jutta wouldn't be responsive at all. But five minutes into the conversation, it was as if the illness had been swept away. Obviously, her body still did not move, but that was irrelevant. The whole air vibrated, and Jutta's eyes sparkled with impish humor and radicality. This radicality was new to me, and I wanted to keep getting to know it. At the time, I explained it to myself with the idea that her soul was intact – battered, perhaps, but absolutely alive. That this soul raised itself above the body, not only in the decision – a drastic one, especially for those around her – to let it die without mitigating treatment, but also in life. G. W. F. Hegel says that we are spiritual beings.[5] Somehow, we must be able to hold onto that. But without it tipping into superiority toward other living beings, without the integrity of the spirit being measured according to its control over the body – let alone its hostility to pleasure – and above all, without repressing death. Perhaps hunger is a good criterion for finite vitality. Jutta's spirit, at any rate, was hungry. In fact, she epitomized hunger for knowledge. Her university – she had never been to a real one – was the radio. It was on all day, with programs about current affairs and culture. She wanted to fill her vanishing time with as much world as possible.

Was Jutta free? In the Stoic school, a movement which flourished during the fall of Attic democracy, freedom is understood as an exercise in self-control. Faced with the vicissitudes of history, with foreign rule, or even with enslavement, it helps – according to stoicism – to be sure of one's inner freedom. Our attitude to things cannot be dictated by anyone. Thus, when we are faced with the fear of loss, or with other fears, we can rob them of their power by liberating ourselves from them inwardly. Going by the numbers of clicks on YouTube, this worldless notion of freedom is booming again in our neoliberal proto-apocalypse. The most extreme test of any Stoic has always been whether he is able to remain entirely calm in the face of his own death. Only a few have passed this test; Socrates is regarded as an exemplary exception. If that is the criterion, Jutta certainly demonstrated enormous freedom, through all her years of affirming the cup of hemlock.

However, I do not want to be too quick to present Jutta's response to her fate as a choice. What if her death drive was simply greater than her fear of death? Unquestionably, she excelled at taking delight in destruction to a degree that was downright demonic. When the woodshed burned down and her husband was fighting alongside the village fire brigade to extinguish the blaze, she rolled her wheelchair to the window, lit a cigarillo, which she always smoked with a cigarette holder because of her reduced fine motor skills, and watched in glee as the building collapsed in a fountain of sparks. "Like Emperor Nero," said my mother later, in amazement. And in a way, perhaps that was better proof of Jutta's freedom than her equanimity in the face of death: In the time that remained to her, she was able to ensure that she was royally amused. Though a wheelchair is not exactly a throne. That came up once, on one of our first visits. We brought extra chairs to the dinner table, so that everyone would have a seat. Jutta said: "I'm already sitting very comfortably," and indicated her wheelchair, from which she was scarcely able to lift herself any longer. At which my father frowned and said: "I doubt that. And you don't have to pretend out of politeness." Jutta chuckled in acknowledgment.

Jutta spoke quite openly about dying; she was nominally a Christian but did not believe in heaven, hell, or resurrection. She wanted to know exactly what I thought about this topic. I said something about the body as an instrument and the soul as its sound, and how, yes, one could remember the music, and, yes, it ended with the end of the musical instrument – but, purely theoretically, if there were something like two mountain ranges, between which the echo would be thrown back and forth after the performance had ended, then it would still survive, wouldn't it? She said that was a very nice idea, but no, the echo would be at best a very brief reverberation.

In fact, I found the thought of Jutta's death unbearable. Years earlier, I had lost my childhood faith by promising myself that I would pray every day for her to get better. And that failed, in several ways at once. She did not get better – but nor did I pray every day. And because of that, because of the idea that there could be such a responsibility, that someone's recovery could be dependent on someone else's discipline in praying, I began to question all these connections. When Jutta died, six months after my father, there was at least plenty of music in the room. For a whole week, people took turns to stay beside her. The familiar smell of the house – books, smoke, and the Baltic Sea – mixed with the fumes of morphine and all our breath, which made the air oppressive. It seems to me that when we have been eaten away by salt water, there is a way of holding onto each other that means that we don't have to be afraid of the mud. Jutta's spirit did not come back.

Xanthippe was right. On the day of his execution, Socrates saw his friends for the last time. No offense to poor feverish Plato, but although he may have come up with a reasoning to show that not everything depends on life, this leads us to a philosophical cul-de-sac. Even in the dialogue itself, it doesn't entirely seem to convince any of Socrates' companions. As soon as his legs begin to be paralyzed by the hemlock, they start to weep after all. And their teacher's next strategy to convince them is not the argument of dialectics – that death and life always alternate, and death cannot claim to last forever – nor is it the argument of ideas – that the soul must have lived before, otherwise it would not recognize anything – or the argument of essence – that the soul must be unchangeable, otherwise it could not rule over the body. None of that has worked. The argument, if it is an argument, with which Socrates puts a stop to the mourning, is as follows: "What conduct is this, you strange men! I sent the women away chiefly for this very reason, that they might not behave in this absurd way; for I have heard that it is best to die in silence."[6] It works; the men swallow their tears, ashamed.

Let Socrates have his final wish for silence. But Plato's glorification of this silence as an infinite onward journey cannot be the last word. If we want to understand what it means that for a while, when we are living, thinking bodies, we can be free, it does not help us. Or only barely. Plato allows us to grasp a lasting temptation. In the face of death – or rather, when he is hiding from the prospect of dying – he invents a more grandiose variant of the freedom to stay. The possibility, at least for philosophers, of staying forever. With this, time is undermined. Freedom is made not temporal, but eternal. This allows us to see past death and to relativize our lifespan to the point of unimportance. Measured against infinity, even a hundred years of life are nothing but a short walk before being killed by radiation on Mars. It is difficult to stay with Xanthippe. But Plato pays a catastrophic price for his stance: life on earth becomes meaningless to him.

The position of ownership

If my young friend were to study philosophy one day, he would probably soon learn about the distinction, in the history of philosophy, between "negative" and "positive" freedom. Negative freedom is a concept that comes quite close to his longing for Mars – being able to follow our goals unimpeded, without being held back by external constraints. Thus, in this context, "negative" does not mean "bad," but indicates that freedom is defined by the absence of something else. In this case, the absence of constraint. Positive freedom, on the other hand, means that there is a particular guiding idea of how one should live one's life – such as Socrates' recommendation that one should be in control of one's desires and concentrate on the philosophical search for truth. Thus, there is something through which we can reach freedom. Freedom would then be progress on the right path, and not the idea that all paths were always open. The inventor of this terminology, the British liberal Isaiah Berlin, was quite sure that any positive definition of this kind would lead to paternalism, and thus ultimately to a lack of freedom: "Once I take this view, I am in a position to ignore the actual wishes of men or societies, to bully, oppress; torture them in the name, and on behalf, of their 'real' selves."[7] For Berlin, only negative freedom can be relied upon as freedom. Other positions, more strongly influenced by Hegel or by feminism, counter this by arguing that it is wrong to conclude that bullying would result from the external proposal of a definition. Emancipatory positions of positive freedom do not dictate any particular approach to life. They confirm the value of negative freedom but emphasize that without a preexisting social world, there cannot be any individual who has desires or makes choices.[8] The individual must have been raised by someone, looked after by someone. Education, laws, care – the institutions and infrastructures that mediate all of this are social, but that does not necessarily make them limiting. Likewise, the options we choose between in a concrete situation arise from a shared world and not from pure fantasy. And even when it comes to fantasy: our language and interpretative patterns are culturally learned. From the viewpoint of positive freedom, social guidelines or interlocutors are thus not always only potential hindrances, let alone impositions. On the contrary, it is only through them that we achieve freedom at all. Rather than turning away from the world to philosophize, or setting off for a planet of our own, freedom lovers should therefore turn to earthly politics and work together to create the conditions most conducive to freedom.

Let us see what my future colleague says to that. To me, it seems that this contrast is not yet satisfactory. Much as the defense of positive freedom appeals to me, it does create a new puzzle. How exactly should we interpret that part about the conditions of freedom? Looked at more closely, the argument divides into two very different variants. Either we mean something obvious and tangible: Freedom has conditions. It does not exist in a vacuum. If you want to be free without paying attention to these conditions, you are irrational. Almost all liberals today see it that way. But if we don't just want to insist self-righteously that a child needs oxygen, soup, and the warmth of a nest, our heads will soon start to spin. If this twelve-year-old is to be able to look forward to lovely years of freedom when he reaches retirement age, we have to do a lot more than cook for him and bring him up properly. We'd have to change everything on the spot. And the living situation of this child himself would change drastically if we were serious about the idea that the freedom of all citizens of the world is just as important as his. Soon, it becomes harder to see freedom beyond all the conditions. That is what we are experiencing at the moment in all liberal societies: In the thicket of demands, required for the maintenance of general freedom, the cohesion of liberal freedom is lost. Many people leave reason behind and proclaim the freedom of phantom possession. Others, who want to remain socially liberal, no longer insist on autonomy but advocate reason directly – or even the value of sacrifice.[9]

But there is a second alternative, when it comes to understanding the defense of positive freedom. It is dizzying in a different way. Because this argumentation rests on an idea that is truly unfamiliar to us in the world of competition and harassment. It is a Hegelian idea, and Karl Marx formulated it particularly well when he said that emancipation from bourgeois society meant that every human being should find in others not the limit, but the "realisation [. . .] of his own freedom."[10] This means that my freedom would not end where the freedom of others began but would grow in conjunction with their freedom. If that is true, no place would be less free than Mars. From this perspective, what would be missing in space, preventing our freedom, would be other people and all the institutions connecting us with each other. Here, the positive notion of freedom is deeply social, as Xanthippe described the unfreedom of death: "This is the last time now that your friends will speak to you or you to them." This mutuality – that is, being the interlocutor of someone else who is just as free as we are, and who is able to relate reciprocally to us and our needs – is the kernel of the communist idea. That is truly a different idea from the one which was enforced through state terror, and which confirmed Isaiah Berlin's concern regarding any kind of positive freedom. But even this idea, that really everyone should be free and should mutually support each other's freedom, is too small a dream for the tasks we are facing now. Because in social freedom, it is still only other people who are missing on Mars. What about the swallows, what about the earth, what should we do about the fact that even wind and weather are now an effect of human labor? We cannot just add that into our model. We cannot declare the whole cosmos to be our reciprocal interlocutor. It might sound nice, but hardly anyone really believes it. And this view also obscures the particular responsibility that falls to the human species, with its special way of being free. We can understand other species' conditions of life and intervene in them more deliberately than swallows and salt water do in ours. If, however, we add in the earth according to the first alternative – understanding freedom in the context of conditions that must be taken into account – we again have the mess of overwhelming conditions. So many new obligations, so little freedom. Who wouldn't want to escape into space?

It seems to me that a positive ecological freedom only becomes tangible – less fairytale, less overwhelming – when we start again from the other end and also look at negative freedom differently. Because that is where the actual mistake is hidden. This notion of just being able to do whatever we want arbitrarily, without anyone getting in the way: that is not merely negative. Having everything fully at our disposal does not simply result from an absence of constraint. It is a very particular idea, mediated by a specific image, and thus in its own sense a positive freedom: the freedom of the modern property owner.

In 1962, Isaiah Berlin's contemporary, the political philosopher Crawford Macpherson, produced an influential interpretation of the early modern contract theorists, the thinkers with whom the tradition of negative freedom originates. Macpherson emphasizes that Thomas Hobbes, John Locke, and their radical contemporaries, such as the English "Levellers," not only created a new understanding of political community but also a whole new figure: the freeborn individual who entered into the social contract. He is, in comparison with the surrounding serfs, enslaved people, maids, laborers, apprentices, children, and wives, a glorious being: the free individual is independent and equal to his brothers. Macpherson calls this subject of the whole liberal tradition the "possessive individual." "Possessive" does not only stand for the fact that free citizens had a right to hold property in their own names. Possessive individualism pertains to the relationship of the individual to himself, in the sense that he is the owner of himself. That is what defines his freedom: not belonging to anyone else and not having to owe anyone anything for that.[11] Freedom as self-ownership, then: in the history of ideas, that is the great alternative to Plato's search for freedom in the ideal conduct of life. Self-ownership, as already mentioned, is no neutral or unconditional starting point for freedom. Far from being the mere absence of coercion, possessive individualism mediates freedom through a social given: the institution of modern property. It seems to me unavoidable that freedom is mediated, that it must be more than the absence of something. Proving that self-ownership, too, is a positive definition of freedom is thus not in itself a criticism. But let us look at what this particular mediation of freedom does with time.

In a certain way, possessive individualism is also a conception of the freedom to stay, but one in which time is suppressed in precisely the opposite way to *Phaedo*'s version. Instead of being lost in eternity, it is chopped up into a perpetual present. That is a surprising finding because at first sight everything in early contract theory seems to point to an awareness of mortality. Thomas Hobbes can be accused of many things, but he certainly wouldn't have left Xanthippe in the lurch. Quite the opposite: he himself declared the reality of death to be the inner impulse driving his whole political philosophy. In his autobiography, he states that his mother actually gave birth to twins: himself and fear. The shock of the Spanish Armada, which attacked England in May 1588, apparently caused her to go into labor prematurely. And fear then motivated Hobbes' new justification of governmental power as a guarantee against civil war. Everything is designed to wrest from mortality some possibility of staying in a certain security: at least not having to die a premature, violent death. Hobbes certainly would not have accepted his death sentence stoically; instead, he spent parts of his life in exile in Paris to avoid getting caught between the fronts in the English civil war. Unlike Socrates, he managed to reach his nineties. The fear of death, then, is something with which the non-stoic possessive individual is all too familiar. And yet, in a hidden way, death in itself, as individual mortality, is shifted out of view.

This operation succeeds by imagining freedom in terms of space. Fear, as Hobbes articulates it, projects all danger onto a sudden external attack. The individual life which is to be protected is a piece of property: the body as a belonging, which can only be moved by its rightful owner. Thus, freedom is not viewed over the course of time but repeatedly assessed anew, in the given moment. As if it were a geometric measurement, assessing freedom involves asking what kind of scope there is right now to put one's will into action without damage. Hidden from view is the question of whether all these individual moments connect together into a lifetime spent in a way that makes sense, or what kind of relationship they have with the flourishing of others, or even whether the various isolated possibilities are actually beneficial to one's own future. From this bird's eye view, focusing on our scope for movement, we cannot see the sequences that follow. If we only measure the space of the present, we make death invisible. At some point it then comes along, as a surprise attack, and we're not forearmed – but then it's all over anyway.

Hobbes, like the era in which he lived, was officially Christian – and the civil war that was raging was about the question of denomination, which was connected with succession to the throne – but his suppression of death is very much of this world. It is still prevalent today. Its connection with property blasts freedom out of time. And not only does possessive individualism fail to see death, but it shifts it permanently onto others. Even without needing to. If freedom means allowing the tyranny of the property owner to rule in limited spheres, then it always has an object. There must be something for the subject to rule over, in order to feel free at any given moment. If things take their proper course, this experience should play out within the individual self. But having full power over one's own body is quite an unstable relationship. Where is the boundary? Doesn't it mean that every time we break into a sweat or find ourselves shivering, that makes a mockery of our self-control? The real possessive individual never ruled only in relation to himself. The citizen of early modern times had a house and an estate and a wife and servants, and could assert his will in relation to them. When unpropertied workers began to be regarded as sovereign individuals, they enjoyed the contrast to enslaved people, who were declared unfree by racist categorization. Husbands possessed an external sphere – clearly defined contractually – that was at their mercy, marked out in the flesh and the work of their wives. And now, where in democratic societies emancipation is supposedly complete and all citizens are entitled to the status of fully valid people, each of us reigns despotically over things in a manner unheard of in world history. Almost everything we buy – in order to live, or in order to pass the time or to rig out our existence with trophies – is attached to bits of nature,

nature that has been dominated to death. Possessive individualism has always relied on phantom property: on the fathomless demand to place parts of the living world fully at our own mercy. Thus, liberal freedom has its source in a strange mixture of the fear of death and its denial, a mixture which has the effect of endlessly reenacting death. Something else must be dead so that I can then experience my freedom through it. Alone on Mars, the setting guarantees that the environment does not stir. Among the teeming masses on earth, such lifelessness must be brought about through violence: by using the geometry of property rights to mark out particular areas of life, and allowing them to be used freely without interruption.

Mediation through property allows liberal freedom to disregard life and withdraw from time. The attempt to move away from this and think about individual freedom differently, in temporal terms, connects our highest capacity back to the limited length of our lives. We only have unconstrained time as long as we live and are well provided for. If the length of our lifetime forms the starting point for freedom, we cannot get around death. The individual who *possesses* denies death and banishes it recklessly to other bodies. The individual who *stays* must face the reality of death.

Seeing death

"I have always regarded this to be one of the inviolable terms of our existence," writes the essayist Kathryn Schulz: "The people we love cease to exist upon death, as definitively as water flows out of a glass when you overturn it."[12] This confronts us with mortality as an unalterable fact. But it is not easy to find a clear-sighted approach to this fact, particularly in a culture that relies so strongly on shifting death somewhere else. If death is mentioned in our everyday lives, there is often a sense of awkwardness. As if something obscene has been said. Embarrassed silence, or a frenetic torrent of words, which refers entirely to the speakers' discomfort with their own deaths. Empty phrases rain down, husks of words and thoughtless advice. Or the silence stretches out into utter horror. Don't start on that, I can't deal with that right now. Mentioning the fact that someone close to us is terminally ill or dying often resembles a hellish kind of coming out. Usually, we give the information not so much because we really need to talk about it but because of the need to bring a bit of consistency into what we say. We just want to be able to tell the truth when someone asks, "Where were you on the weekend?" or "What do your parents do?" My mum runs a farm; my father is – dying. It sounds so stupid. Even though all of us do it.

Jutta, so it seemed with the grace of middle distance, continuously died one long death, which she wanted to outwit by giving much more ground to its conditions than would have been necessary. What was crazy about my father's process of dying was the escalation. Usually, deciding to fight for our lives does not increase the possible ways of dying. In this case, it did. An incomplete list of the so-called therapy-related secondary illnesses he suffered as a result of his leukemia includes fungal infection, pulmonary bleeding, coma, epilepsy, psychosis, edema, loss of the immune system, and multiple months of febrile delirium. Each one of them presented him with a different death – or, in one instance, made him contemplate murder. And through it all, my father fought a desperate fight for freedom in the form of control over the situation. Death – the high likelihood that he would die – was never considered a part of that, even when he was discharged twice (!) by the doctors to die at home. I still blame myself for this, but it really seemed impossible to take away any of the horror of this option by mentioning it. Obviously, I blame him for it all the more. But for him, death meant only defeat, and he didn't believe in defeat.

On the other hand, I am glad that my dad never fobbed us off with Platonic comfort. And at least once, we must have ended up talking about death after all. Because I can still remember how – probably also to avoid the topic of burial – he said, "Well, the best thing would be for the wolves to eat me, then at least someone would get something out of it." I still find this moving. But other than that, it was high treason even to catch oneself implying anything that didn't suggest that victory was absolutely assured.

Given the contempt his own parents had shown for any sign of weakness, the fact that my father did not hide the physical ravages of his illness was already quite an emancipation. But the solution of claiming that this was only the illness and not a trace of mortality also came at a considerable price. The claim to immortality required a bitter struggle for control over the situation. For the whole decade of his illness, and through all his stays at the clinic, my father tried to defy the constraints of treatment. This meant only eating food from home, always taking household remedies at the same time as the prescribed medicine, hearing about everything that was going on in the life he was missing and making all of it his business – and also making everything that happened in his own life the business of everyone else. The warlike mood rubbed off on me; at least at the start, I was a glowing aide-de-camp in his campaign, later I became a deserter for a while, and in the end, I came back again after all.

For me, the image of "seeing death and not being allowed to see it" will always be the moment when my father woke up in intensive care from an artificially induced coma. After the ventilation tubes were taken out, he could not speak. Nor did he quite seem to be there. It was one of the moments when my mother and I were both there at the same time. Saliva was constantly running out of his mouth, and we wiped it away using the rough paper towels that you find in hospitals and in petrol station toilets. He wanted us to do it differently. It was about the angle at which we were holding the paper towels, and he seemed to feel that we should fold them differently. We didn't understand. It felt like hours. Again and again, he pushed away the paper towels, his hands still stiff, emaciated, and drew shapes in the air in slow motion, like instructions for a craft project. We still didn't understand. Maybe there wasn't even anything to understand. Maybe it was just the empty shell of a gesture, directing something. But that shifting gaze, the wretched and fearful helplessness that could suddenly flare up, tipping into the deepest contempt for our incompetence, that was death.

I actually wanted to give that as an example for a particular temporal structure: the suppression of death in the effort to control a certain moment. But it also shows that in this case of making freedom spatial and chopping up time into whichever present time needs to be controlled at that moment, it was not only about a precautionary paranoia, or a vain escape from temporality and general mortality. My father was really dying. In the fight against the illness, he became tyrannical in various ways and even seriously considered extending his fate to us. But he was exposed to a situation, and we were exposed to him in that situation, which no one should experience. Everything depends on the fact that it is also possible to die differently.

Initially, it seemed to me that Jutta's case, in comparison with ours, was a clear example of a successful death. With more distance, the contrast is leveled out. Both of them – and who can blame them? – used the terror of death. Jutta's freedom consisted precisely in her refusal to allow treatment to disturb her process of dying. In her way, she also passed death on despotically to her surroundings. Those around her had no choice. And I was perhaps just not close enough to see this death in more facets or in more depth. Both are borderline cases. In such cases, it might be appropriate to disregard the freedom to stay and resort to a more extreme variant. But that cannot be the paradigm for a whole life; it is the wrong pattern, and nor is it effective as a precaution. At worst, attempting not to have to see death, and to conceive of freedom as freedom from death, leads to a multiplication of death. Death pervades freedom. Freedom begins to love death. Or even becomes deadly. We no longer see death because we see with death's eyes. And ultimately, we also do that as caregiving families, as people who in our society – pending a care revolution – are absolutely irreplaceable and absolutely overburdened. The presumption of immortality in the denial of death is met – when the exhaustion is great enough – with the wish for an immediate end. We see with death's eyes: Just die, so that I can be free again! This is worse than confronting the unbearableness of death: realizing that its unbearableness is wearing off.

Seeing death in the "right" way, if there is such a thing, means confronting both at the same time: its unbearableness and its immutability. And this mixture, outlandish as it might sound, is actually a great boon. Unbearable and immutable. Seen like that, death is not a bitter limit on the freedom to stay, which we have to accept with gritted teeth as the horizon of our temporal perspective. It is practically a mercy. Unbearable, meaning that it breaks our deep connections with each other and with life itself. Immutable, meaning that it's nobody's fault.

We treat far too many deaths as bearable. Plenty of lives pass and are seen as dispensable or "ungrievable."[13] And for plenty of people, life is unlivable. Mortality is immutable in general, but plenty of real deaths could be avoided. My father may have wished to meet his end among wolves, in the state of nature, as it were. But the fact that he became incurably ill with cancer at the age of forty-one was probably because of his position in the division of labor in society. Summer after summer with only three hours of sleep per night: watering the fields can only be done at night, without sunlight, and close to the Danish border it is only dark for a few hours in June. And during his apprenticeship, it was quite usual to prepare carcinogenic pesticides without protective clothing. For many older men outside the upper classes, that is the mask worn by death: uncomplaining drudgery without being a sissy. For others, death wears the face of the police cell, the car's bonnet, the jealous ex-partner, too much schnapps or too much sugar. Air pollution or total exhaustion: death, when it comes into view, is a strange mixture of luck and class. The scandal is not that we die in the first place. As unbearable as it is, we can't change that. The scandal is that some of us die so much younger than others. It is not simply that some lives are better protected from death, although that is of course the case, and will be as long as there is a pharma industry and a class society. But class also means that the protection of the better-off consists of attacks on the unprotected. Class means that humanity is so divided that it repeats within itself what otherwise only applies to external nature: that all life lives on other lives. Humans are the only species that sets up its own conditions, meaning that even in a thoroughly cannibalistic nature, it could be obliged to show mercy. Instead of that, we are the only species to organize things in such a way that the lives of a very few depend on the early deaths of the many. And that is not only the case in the exceptional circumstances of war, but also in what we call peace. In real peace, death would look different. Each death would be unbearable. Each death would be unavoidable because at worst it would have been brought about by an actual accident, but not compelled too early by badly arranged social structures.

Looking ahead peacefully at death does not require us to reconcile ourselves all that much with dying. On the contrary. Facing death means working against it. That is what work is actually there for, rather than for lining the pockets of the rich and the phantom property owners. It might seem tough to insist on the unbearableness of death. Wasn't it right to say that Xanthippe was too intransigent? Shouldn't philosophy still – at least a little bit – teach us the wisdom of dying? Letting go at the right moment? It seems to me that something like acceptance of mortality precisely doesn't come when we have a direct encounter with death. It is rather a certain view of life that takes the horror out of its finitude: a sense of living abundance that gives cause for gratitude. A sense of overarching connections that will outlast our own lives.

However, that does not make the unavoidable death bearable. After all, we don't survive our own deaths. And we never experience other people's deaths fully: we cannot take on their dying for them, and we can't even feel it with them. Sympathy for the dying is really a category error. Because we don't share the last part with them. The final moment always divides into an end for one and a loss for the others. If it goes well, we can provide support across this gulf: seeing death and standing firm. That, too, would mean staying.

Trillions on Mars

If we look at the relative success of emancipation and democratization, we might think that crude possessive individualism is a relic of the past. Feminist philosophers and daughters might still be going on about it – but isn't it wearing a bit thin by now? Should we just leave Hobbes and his heirs in peace?

In fact, if we take up this concern and move away from the history of ideas to examine the philosophy of those who hold the most power at present, we will find ourselves faced with an even more monstrously outsized property obsession. Longtermism is taught at Oxford and Cambridge and included on lists of *New York Times* bestsellers. The approach leads to billions of dollars of philanthropic spending, it dominates in Silicon Valley, and it is regarded as the creed of Elon Musk, currently the richest man in the world. Obviously, the idea of things being long term sounds good – almost like a plea to think in temporal terms. And the first step in the argumentation does actually respond to our most careful instincts. If I leave a shard of glass on the ground, is it any worse if a child cuts his or her feet on it tomorrow or in a hundred years? This is the question asked by one of the main representatives of longtermism, William MacAskill.[14] And if it's no worse, shouldn't we focus on the long-term effects of our actions, such as the consequences of climate change for future generations? Of course.

Longtermism is a form of utilitarianism, a moral philosophy in which the happiness of the largest number of individuals defines how we should act. Already in its usual form, this approach is known for sadistic thought experiments: if a goods train is heading for a young family and you could divert it onto a different track so that instead it will run over an overweight old man, should you do that? The philosophical innovation of the longtermist approach lies only in the fact that the number of people is detached from their presence. Most people have not lived yet. It is possible that the eight billion who exist right now don't even weigh anything against the number of those to come.

Obviously, that depends on how things go for humanity. So, for longtermists, the duty to ensure the happiness of the greatest number coincides with the duty to ensure the existence of that greatest number in the first place. "Population collapse due to low birth rates is a much bigger risk to civilization than global warming," Elon Musk tweeted in summer 2022, in the middle of the biggest heatwave ever experienced by Europe. And, in fact, that is precisely MacAskill's argument: Climate change may be a problem for humanity, but not a very crucial one since it is likely – in his view – that the survivors will adapt and population numbers will recover.[15] That is also why he argues that part of our oil reserves should be left untouched – not to stop global warming, but so that industrial civilization can be built up again after it collapses.[16] If you now think that the number of people who are sitting unhappily on the rails waiting for the train to run them over will end up being quite high, then your thinking is not long term enough. The moral shock of playing out potential human lives against real living humans who are feeling joy and pain and planning their futures is large enough. But this notion of the long term is one that does not care about the world itself, either. Whether the swallows come back is just as irrelevant as the question of whether the Amazon rainforest survives, or whether there will be lakes we can swim in. Nothing has to remain, except for humanity. And even that is hard to recognize in the image of the future painted by longtermism.

For the enormous number of those born afterward, compared to whom every current disaster can be neglected, is not supposed to result only from the length of time being imagined. Inspired by science fiction and the futurist Ray Kurzweil, the main representative of longtermism, Nick Bostrom, is betting on a so-called "singularity."[17] This refers to an "intelligence explosion" in AI research, which would enable exponential population growth and usher in the posthuman age favored by Bostrom. The crucial factor in that would be the development of computer-assisted brain simulations so complete that in a network of "uploaded" existences, they would count as people.[18] Virtually powered individuals could then be varied and multiplied with the ease of software copies. A side effect of this would be the fulfillment of the masculinist dream of entirely taking over the power to give birth. Added to this comes the nightmare of human optimization, resulting in a digital form of eugenics.

Bostrom paints a picture of various kinds of "progress," which individually or together could characterize the posthuman age: most people would have almost entire control over their sensory experiences, the majority of humans would be far more intelligent than they are today, psychological suffering would hardly exist anymore, life expectancy would be over five hundred years and the population would rise to more than a trillion.[19] As predictions, these vague fantasies are obviously bizarre, but they reveal striking patterns of thought: phantom possession over one's own body is expanded to its experiences and the length of its life. We are supposed to be able to control everything that manages to touch us. The resistance of a world shared with others would simply bounce off the surface of these monads in their shells. And the inevitability of death would be revoked. Bostrom himself wears a bracelet with precise instructions to the firm Alcor, which specializes in the preservation of corpses. After his death, his body is to be placed in an enormous steel capsule filled with liquid nitrogen. This means that he should be able to be reanimated when the technology for computer-simulated continued living is finally developed.[20]

For the longtermist, the greatest evils we have to fight are so-called existential risks such as nuclear war, out-of-control robot armies, and bioweapons. What makes a risk existential is again unrelated to our current existence. It is the prevention of the possibility of reaching posthuman conditions and – this is referred to explicitly – colonizing space.[21] If we follow this definition, an environmental movement which limited the use of rocket fuel would present a greater existential risk than climate change itself. Existential risks may be described as tragic accidents in human history as a whole, but if we remember the container of liquid nitrogen, we begin to get the impression that this is really about those scenarios in which the corpses of individual super-rich longtermists cannot be thawed and reanimated.

What is there to say? Compared with this, Hobbes was a harmless innocent. Or a prophet. That is how Hannah Arendt read him. Her famous study of totalitarianism contains an analysis of the Hobbesian axioms which ends up looking a lot grimmer than Macpherson's theory of possessive individualism.[22] Arendt, too, emphasizes that modern bourgeois society subordinated its political categories to the paradigm of property. But she is less interested in property in the self than in the form of labor that can be sold. Her focus is on the new, early capitalist accumulation function of property: that its meaning lies in its multiplication. Accumulation is growth defined by purely quantitative aspects, meaning not the growth of a child into an adult, but the growth from a hundred to a thousand specimens. What *Leviathan* shows, according to Arendt, is that property accumulation cannot succeed without a parallel accumulation of power. As the guarantee of the conditions of increasing property, the bourgeois state is thrown into an imperialist spiral of expansion: "Only by acquiring more power can it guarantee the status quo; only by constantly extending its authority and only through the process of power accumulation can it remain stable."[23] In so far as possessive individualism has created a freedom that can only be grasped as geometrical space to move at any given moment, the process of accumulation now reintroduces time. But it is a time built on the model of capitalist property: the time of the bare process of growth. For Arendt, the core of totalitarianism is the domination that declares such a process to be a political goal in itself, and subordinates all human action to that purpose. And she sees every such process as heading for catastrophe:

> The imperialist-minded businessman, whom the stars annoyed because he could not annex them, realized that power organized for its own sake would beget more power. When the accumulation of capital had reached its natural, national limits, the bourgeoisie understood that only with an "expansion is everything" ideology, and only with a corresponding power-accumulating process, would it be possible to set the old motor into motion again.[24]

At first glance, what distinguishes longtermism from more familiar fascism is that there is no specific group predestined to build the *Reich* of eternal domination. But, at second glance, there obviously is. Because it follows from the connection of the future with techno-fantastical innovation that certain lives in the present are infinitely more valuable than others. The wellbeing of textile workers and day laborers is practically irrelevant to the happiness of the coming trillions, whereas an engineer at a tech giant could bring about the singularity. From this, another leading light of longtermism, Nick Beckstead, concludes in his doctoral thesis in philosophy that it is more important to protect a life in a rich country than a life in a poor one.[25] For Arendt, the project of subordinating the plurality and spontaneity of humanity's living together to an overarching historical process would already be totalitarian: seeing humanity altogether only as a vehicle of its own accumulation already presents the specter of its superfluity. The logic of increase creates nothing that lives on, nothing to hold our memory. Increase is basically a competition in which the next moment always outdoes the previous one. As soon as there is something bigger, what came before is unnecessary. Just as all life existing right now is worthless in comparison with the speculative fantasy of the "intelligence explosion."

In longtermism, the motifs of a dystopian kind of staying are brought together and pushed to extremes: immortality and possessive individualism. Not souls but silicon will conquer death. And continued life in a fiberglass world without mud or salt water is imagined as a megalomaniac power over everything: phantom possession of the universe. However, actual talk of freedom is suspiciously rare in this vision. At most, it comes up in relation to overcoming death and disturbing sensory impressions (such as criticism, perhaps). But neither the hoarding of "humanity" nor the hoarding of "property" can overcome finitude. Both only expand the shadow of death to the whole of life, in which nothing counts any longer but the hunt for antidotes. Hobbes' *Leviathan* and Bostrom's lab are monuments to a desperate search to banish the fear of death without having to face one's own mortality.

Staying here, staying mortal

If we see freedom in terms of time, that means first of all that those who have a longer life have more freedom. How could that not be the case? The longer we are able to do things, the greater our freedom. Death is the end of freedom, and that is exactly why we don't want to die. The freedom to stay means being able to go on living. It means that it matters whether an eighty-year-old heart patient lives through one more spring, or two, or three. At the beginning of the pandemic, my mother sometimes said to customers who got upset about wearing a mask, "Have you ever seen an intensive care ward with patients on ventilators? If I can spare one single person from being artificially respirated, I'm happy to wear a mask for the rest of my life. And you have to do it too, at least in my shop." That is the concrete variation of the reaction I have when I hear those who opposed pandemic policies as somehow "unnatural," saying that our society is in denial about death. There is more than one kind of denial. Saying "people die all the time" can be an even more serious kind of denial than the ways in which we cover it up by believing in immortality or geometrical spheres of tyrannical freedom. Because it means behaving as if all suffering were equally unavoidable, and as if the unbearableness of death were made up.

So, the first important point is being able to stay at all, but that is not all. Because, at the same time, in order to be free, this life has to be experienced from the position of staying, and not just become mired in a desperate fight to fend off death. That seems to me to be the deeper meaning of Jutta's "spirituality," what I now understand as a lesson. I am grateful for that lesson in the way that we are grateful for salvation, and not merely for a present. What showed itself through her, this sparkling vitality despite the beginning of paralysis, was not an immortal soul. But it was a freedom: the freedom not to be led by the fear of death, not to subordinate everything – and, with that, freedom itself – to that fear. Jutta went right to the extreme of refusing possible treatments, but to me that doesn't seem to be the most essential point. The essence was in creating unconstrained time, without having to deny mortality. Unconstrained time that would be the alternative to supposedly negative freedom as a space free of interruptions – and thus modelled on property. Staying as the first stage of freedom. And an abundance of time as its realization.

The freedom to stay, which neither dissolves time into eternity nor into fragments of the present, must hold onto finitude. Anyone who wants to remain here will see death: its unbearableness, its inevitability. Even under the prevailing circumstances, I still harbor this untamable wish that it should be possible to face the reality of death. Even in its unbearable bearableness and its avoidable unavoidability. Ensuring that the time we have left is not devastated by death. Would that not be freedom, or at least one of its beginnings?

And yet: doesn't affirming our mortality mean that too much infinity falls away? Even if imagining death becomes acceptable, doesn't the temporal limit curtail freedom too much? Can one seriously write about freedom and blame people for their longing for endless expansion, their longing for the universe? Awful megalomaniac businesspeople aren't the only ones who want to go to Mars. The magnificent Black science fiction author Octavia E. Butler was fascinated by the exploration of Mars, and her prophetic protagonist in *Parable of the Sower* proclaims the aim of humanity several times as follows: "The Destiny of Earthseed / Is to take root among the stars."[26] And the person whom I love most, partly because I'm sure that even in a rocky desert I would never be bored with her, exclaims in outrage: "How can you claim that there isn't anything to see on Mars? It would be so interesting to know more about the structure of minerals there. Whether there's water there after all, traces of life. Why are you assuming that people just want to go to Mars so they can colonize it? Maybe we want to go there to stop idiots like Elon from colonizing it!" "But earth," I say, "is much,

much more beautiful. And here there are millions of species we haven't yet discovered, which will go extinct before we know about them." She stares at me, perplexed. "So? Did I say that we should give up on earth, just because we're interested in Mars? We should get to know all those little beetles. But why shouldn't we also get to know Mars?"

It is not Mars that ruins the freedom to stay. It is the idea of Mars as an empty, dead proto-property. Can we imagine freedom differently? Can we keep death in view as our own end, and still taste something of that infinity, without which freedom loses its flavor?

2
Fulfilled Time

Abundance made scarce

My suggestion that we think about freedom from the perspective of staying shifts freedom from the spatial dimension into a temporal one. In spatial terms, "staying" means stagnation. From a temporal point of view, it at least promises that something will last. But as mortal beings, we do not last forever. That's why it's so tempting to disregard time: because in the end, we can't stay. And the usual concept of freedom does actually ask us to step out of time. It suggests that we should see ourselves as property owners, who always only estimate their own scope for movement at a certain given moment. The freedom to stay rejects that exit from time. It upholds the finite, earthly lifespan and begins by measuring freedom quite simply, according to the length of life.

But merely staying alive is not yet freedom. As important as it is to protest against statistically early deaths caused by social inequality, more time is not in itself already more freedom. On the contrary: it would be cruel to measure freedom simply by counting it on the calendar. If staying alive were the ultimate goal, we shouldn't be occupied with anything other than preparatory and precautionary measures. An early death would then not only be unfortunate but would mean a failed existence. Our struggle for freedom would turn into a competition to outlive each other. That is miserable. And it doesn't make sense. Because time can be as much a curse as a blessing. Someone whose qualifications are worth nothing on the job market could also have plenty of time, as could someone who is refused permission to work by the immigration authorities, or someone who is in prison. They have time, but their time is not free. And even someone who seems on the surface to have plenty of leisure can suffer from depression, meaning that they can have time without it being fulfilled. The freedom to stay is an abundance of time, but it is also much more. We have to define time more precisely, meaning that we should at least speak of "an abundance of free time." But that brings us back to the beginning. Because what do we mean by "free"?

We could simply say that free time is time with which I can do whatever I want. That would basically mean once again applying the model of property as a script for freedom, except that now it is time that belongs to me and not, as in classic possessive individualism, my body. This means that time, which is actually our life, is frozen in its regulated, measurable form. This form is historically no older than factory work or railway timetables. The time that we can decide to use in this way or that way is empty – otherwise, it wouldn't be so movable. This empty time, measured out and ultimately abstract, is the prerequisite for being able to sell our labor in classic wage-labor conditions. It is nothing but duration, packaged together with our own abilities, which are utilized for other people's purposes. If you think that freedom means being able to do what you want with your time, that doesn't change anything about the capitalist form of time. It just means that you transfer the time to yourself. That's not nothing. And yet freedom as ownership of time sounds like a single well-rested person who has various options on a Saturday afternoon, chooses between them and can switch at any time if they get bored. This is certainly one aspect of freedom: the notion that you can sometimes take possession of some time in which you can do as you like without being disturbed. But the fundamental experience of a rich life is rather that your time does not belong to you. Not only because it can end forever at any moment but because you share it with others. Every deeper connection, every long-term plan, every responsibility you take on means that you no longer own your own time. Asking yourself every fifteen minutes "Do I really want this?" is more of a recipe for undermining your own will than for being free. We could obviously say that the formula of "doing what you want with your time" should be understood more broadly. By devoting yourself to lasting connections with others, you are doing what you want. But the fact that you can do that is far less a result of your own control over your time than it is of the fact that your own time has been claimed by others in an agreeable way. We do not fill our time alone. If we like how our time takes shape, that is because our time has a particular quality: it is fulfilled.

Fulfilled time: that seems to me to be a fitting description of freedom. Fulfilled time allows us to stay without becoming unfree. The individual will might be a good referee when it comes to an acute lack of time, but it is not the actual criterion for gaining freedom. Thus, this chapter is about time itself, about the form we give to it. I am looking for a time that is neither empty nor eternal, a time that seems to burst out of its own limits.

Simone de Beauvoir and Hannah Arendt see the key to freedom in the realization of agency and not in the choice between different options. Agency can succeed, in their view, when it makes a connection with the most extreme points in our lives: birth and death. That leaves many things open, but it doesn't leave anything the same. Because fundamentally, these boundary experiences are not points of reference at all: they themselves become models for how we refer and relate to anything in the first place. Through mortality and natality, we can shift everything we do into a light that makes it meaningful or mutable. If that succeeds, mere life is transformed into freedom.

In 1923, Virginia Woolf noted down a resolution in her diary: "I want to make life fuller and fuller."[1] That is how I imagine freedom: making life fuller, making time more fulfilled. I think that is a workable concept. But it also raises plenty of questions. First of all, one could object that this talk of "abundance" and "fulfillment" binds us all the more tightly to the capitalist society of affluence. Freedom as an abundance of fulfilled time? Shouldn't we be moving on from conspicuous consumption? Wouldn't it be better to imagine the freedom to stay as an ascetic ideal? Criticize false needs, call for simple living and degrowth? I think the point is rather to change the temporality that underlies any possible abundance. The timeless freedom of the possessive individual was firmly tied to the temporality of unstoppable historical progress. The society that protected property rights and promised freedom to the individual was dynamic in a specific way. Its development was understood, especially in the nineteenth century, as an ascending line, as continuous progress. This ascending line actually consists of two strands. As in a double helix, the liberal promise of freedom and the industrial process of progress are intertwined. The French philosopher Pierre Charbonnier writes that the freedom of modern societies had made a pact with the productive capacities of the earth.[2] This pact dictated that with the increase in individual freedom, affluence (or abundance, *abondance* in the original French) – the availability and disposability of things – would grow. Freedom – our noble, idealistic value – is material through and through, according to Charbonnier. Freedom of movement, for example, does not simply mean being able to go out of the house but being able to travel using private cars, airlines, and railways. As a historian of ideas, Charbonnier mainly traces how in all key philosophical theories of modern freedom, explicit claims were made about the endlessly expandable exploitation of the earth. But this finding also applies in terms of social psychology because freedom attracts us due to the fact that we can hope for even more from it: prosperity. The modern possessive individual entered an overarching temporality predicated on the escalation logic of colonial and industrial expansion but seen through the rose-tinted glasses of profiteers. It is no wonder that with the realization that growth has limits, classic liberal freedom also starts to flounder. Having in order to have more: Can we emancipate ourselves from that? Can we escape to a different kind of enlightenment which would not conquer the world but release it?

Charbonnier himself implies that decoupling freedom from the promise of abundance could solve the problem. But this abundance contains so much that we cannot simply cut it off while retaining an intact freedom. "Prosperity" also represents the most basic material security, necessary to protect people from hardship. In a market economy, only those people are provided for who can afford to buy products. And without easily accessible and generous social security systems, nothing remains to guarantee the future but one's own property. After all, we don't have access to other people's property, even if they live in entirely unnecessary excess. How should we exercise moderation when we might end up standing alone in the rain? In other words, the wish for abundance is not a separate problem but the more or less desperate reaction to a scarcity created by freedom itself, as long as freedom is tied to property. In contrast, real material abundance would be an unconditional promise that we each have a share in all the basic necessities, as a permanent form of security. But that can only be granted by a different freedom.

And then there is another thing: the difference between affluence, or excess, and abundance. When Charbonnier writes of abundance, he means not only material wealth but boundlessness. The fantasy of capitalist growth aims for an infinite timeline. Having so as to have more, investing so as to be able to invest more: accumulation is endless. It is probably the most pathetic kind of infinity that humans have ever come up with. This apparent fulfillment of the longing for eternity does not discredit every kind of abundance. Rather than letting everyone have a share in wealth, the industrial modern age has destroyed a part of its planetary basis. Beyond whatever property we might have, it is trying to make us get used to a horrendous renunciation of the entire world. Freedom and abundance? Yes, please! Even now, even in the presence of catastrophe, there is still world without end, life in plenty, and there are more human beings than ever. The freedom to stay would mean preserving this abundance, rather than accumulating it out of existence. Can we do that? Can we open the limited span of our lifetimes to this boundlessness – and make life fuller and fuller? I think so, at least if we also free ourselves from the prevailing form of freedom.

Forestalling death

Another of those stubborn Socratic spirits in my life, like Jutta, is Josette. I cannot think of freedom at all without hearing her voice in my head. Years ago, I managed to capture her attention by abruptly claiming that her idea of freedom was that of a prisoner: she just wanted to get out. Since then, we've kept on returning to that topic.

If I think about the last time we talked at length, the first thing I see is darkness. It is a darkness interspersed with glittering light: the lights of Paris, no less. But what struck me was the darkness. It was late October; it didn't only get dark at night, but in the late afternoon. Still, like many other people in autumn 2021, we weren't sitting inside a bistro, but outside, at tables that covered the whole of the sidewalk. Josette had taken the day off and traveled into the city. Spurred on by her skeptical frown, I explained my new idea about freedom being temporal rather than spatial. "I would be more interested in finding out," she interrupted me, "what people actually really mean when they say freedom." "You only want to know that so you can disagree with them," I retorted, "so you can then feel completely free because you're not like other people!" She cocked her head like a bird listening to a sound, rolled her next cigarette without looking down, and did not seem to find my remark worthy of a direct answer. "I am sure," she continued, "that when people say 'freedom', they mean all that consumer shit. They just always want to be able to buy something new." That was positively diplomatic of her: at least we were in agreement on this, as opposed to the "corona shit." "And if they can carry on buying stuff on their phones, they don't mind being locked up." Hmm, maybe not. I would actually have been worried if Josette had learned to be diplomatic. "Don't you think the ability to buy stuff would become less interesting if freedom meant having time? Not owning things but having more life?" I pretty much got the idea from her. She once described a novel she'd read in which the main character – some kind of adventurous sailor – decided to go and visit a friend for two weeks because the friend needed help. When Josette realized that she wouldn't be able to do that, she promptly quit the job she had at the time and got by for quite a while on occasional work. But now her answer was, "You only think that because it works for you." I sighed. "That's why I'm asking you, so that I can work out whether it really only works for me." She relented slightly. "Yes. There is really nothing better than having a free Saturday with nothing on the calendar. A free day ahead of me, no expectation, nothing; I can just see what happens."

A page on the calendar like fresh snow. Freedom as undefined time. Was that the solution? Or was it part of the problem, lacking autonomy in our ordinary working day to such an extent that we end up hating any kind of commitment? I tried to reel off the standard argument against negative freedom – the mere absence of constraint or obligation – on a temporal level: "But a lot of things also become impossible if we just leave time empty, don't they? Wouldn't freedom mean making a plan so you can do what you really want to do?" I was also slightly insulted that our longed-for reunion was now being presented as something that robbed her of her freedom. "Yes, of course we normally make plans. But then it's not that special freedom anymore. It's okay, I wanted it myself, but when it's decided, it ties me down." "Hmm." I chewed on my cold pizza crust. "For me, the days that are most free are the ones when nothing disturbs my routine," I replied. Josette was quite familiar with the shared routines of my household. "Yes. I know," she said. "It seems awful to me. You and your routines, I guess you like it that way, but I wouldn't be able to breathe." I laughed incredulously.

"But you're the one who has a completely fixed daily routine! Didn't I ever tell you? After you were gone, I woke up every morning at five because I couldn't get used to the fact that it was quiet. There was the dawn chorus, but otherwise it was quiet because you weren't sitting under the window on the terrace at sunrise, coughing the soul out of your body, as we say in German." She smiled. "That, my dear, is not routine. That's addiction. That's my body that needs nicotine and coffee."

We rummaged around for change and gave it to the old man who was going from table to table. "Do you know," she began again, "I'm impressed that you can keep to a daily routine like that. I couldn't do it. I don't obey myself." I was fascinated by the image of disobedience to oneself, and I was also a bit confused because I'd been expecting another little dig. "How do you even know," I asked, "that the part that gives orders is the more real version of yourself? The part that wants something else is also you! And when you rebel, you follow that part, don't you?" To be honest, I wouldn't have come up with that response just like that, but I remembered the passage where Hannah Arendt took the idea of the will – a phenomenon that was unknown to ancient philosophy, and which only came to be seen as the center of a person and of freedom in the modern age – and turned it upside down. In *The Life of the Mind*, she writes that without an inner counterpart, the will does not emerge at all. For every *velle*, there is a *nolle*. I want, and I don't want, or I want something different. What we modern people call volition is actually just a trial of strength, won by the stronger tendency, which buries multiple inner voices in an unambiguous action or statement. Arendt weighs up other possibilities for settling the conflict of the will. She writes about love as gravity, or as a counterweight to inner divisions. Perhaps one can imagine that like the current of time, which we share with others and which helps us steer past the rocks of our inner indecision. For Arendt, a free will does not decide alone but can rely on the power of judgment. And the power of judgment is not an inward perspective but a path through various external points of view. Judgment consults the perspectives of others, expanding itself through them, before returning to itself: how will the action look after it has taken place? Afterward, will I want to live with its originator, i.e., myself?[3]

At that moment, Josette was the person I wanted to live with: the Josette I knew, with her virtuoso disobedience to herself. I ordered more wine. She has a hidden way of drawing people into this battle of the wills. Encounters with others are essential to her; for her, there is nothing worse than being stuck in her own perspective – or in her own conflict between perspectives. It is possible to feel as if one is crucial to her, precisely by insisting stubbornly on one's own freedom. That is irresistible. But just as crucial to her is the moment of breaking away. Then, freedom means being independent again, needing no one, and cutting all ties. That, in turn, seemed absolutely unbearable to me. We die anyway; something always happens that we don't have under control, so why do we have to add any extra disturbance to that? Why not just stay together? That was the argument about freedom that I conducted with Josette in my head, whenever she wasn't there. At some point, I realized that of course that could also be a way of cheating death, along with all other uncontrollable vicissitudes: doing something ourselves to keep things moving. Even her next cigarette could be understood that way, scoffing at death: Anything you can do, I can do better!

Getting ahead of death by using its own means but without denying our own mortality – maybe that encapsulates the temporal freedom that we've been looking for? That is the approach of the French philosopher Simone de

Beauvoir, who sat in Parisian cafés in broad daylight in the last century. As an existentialist, Beauvoir sees individual freedom as an unassailable fact. Our consciousness of ourselves forces us into freedom: we must wish, plan, and decide. This entails that we are responsible for our lives. If we hide from this freedom, we live dishonestly, and in a way not as ourselves. We have to face our freedom in order to live our lives. In existentialism, everyone realizes their own freedom by pursuing projects in which they go beyond their current selves – "transcend themselves," as it is called in the terminology developed by Simone de Beauvoir's partner Jean-Paul Sartre. Such projects can be intentions, relationships, or entire life plans. It is from the structure of the project that existentialism derives its temporality: freedom points beyond the moment; it relates not only to the next action that is to be completed but to the projection of a freedom that has to be grasped. However, Beauvoir sees very clearly that we cannot all just start freely making plans. On the contrary: the starting point of every plan is the situation of the individual. No two situations are the same, but to a large extent they are all historically and socially shaped. We don't choose our situation, we find ourselves in it. And even if we're certainly not all sitting in prison, Josette is basically right: we are not free yet. Talking about the freedom to stay sounds almost like a cruel joke. We would first have to be free at all.

Beauvoir discussed women's lack of freedom in her most important work, *The Second Sex*, in a groundbreaking analysis. She sees the fundamental dilemma of the patriarchy in the fact that male domination has ensured that women are unable to define themselves or their own projects. Women serve as a waystation for male freedom but are themselves cut off from transcendence. They remain stuck in their shapeless lives, in an unfreedom that Beauvoir calls "immanence" – they are enclosed in themselves; "an attempt is made to freeze her as an object and doom her to immanence, since her transcendence will be forever transcended by another essential and sovereign consciousness."[4] Immanence is a state which falsely entices us to stay; a staying without freedom. Emancipation from it is, for Beauvoir, a similar act to the maintenance of freedom: it is achieved by going beyond the given situation in one's own projects – but against greater resistance. Transcendence is like entering time. Rather than being trapped as an object in timeless passivity, the subject insists on beginning its own history. "Transcendence" may sound like a rather dramatic expression for the act of shaping one's own life, but the hint of a life after death is crucial to the existentialist position. Every free action – and this applies all the more to those that have to rise up out of oppression – has a bit of death mixed in. The subject negates its current situation and risks its life in some sense, at least the old life, but also the new one since we cannot yet know whether it will succeed.

With its consciousness of time, Beauvoir's existentialism also takes account of death, which is after all unavoidable in temporal approaches to freedom. Beauvoir regards death with an ambivalence by far exceeding the unbearable inevitability described in the previous chapter. For her, death is unacceptable, while at the same time being absolutely necessary. In short: When we die, we cannot make any further plans, but if we never died, all plans would be meaningless.

The first variant, the unacceptability of the end, is described by Beauvoir in a report on her dying mother's time in hospital. The autobiographical text is entitled *A Very Easy Death*. On the one hand, that conveys Beauvoir's bitterly ironic take on the medical procedures which do not foster any kind of ease. "One is caught up in the wheels and dragged along, powerless in the face of specialists' diagnoses, their forecasts, their decisions. The patient becomes their property: get him away from them if you can!"[5] On the other hand, there also seems to be a pretense of "ease" fabricated and upheld by the daughter herself. She seems to underestimate the extent to which she, too, took control of her mother to ensure that she would, according to Beauvoir's rules, die an "easy" death – that is, an unexpected one. The notion that the sick should not be upset or worried unnecessarily was still more common in the sixties, but she takes it to an extreme. Although the diagnosis is clear, she leads her mother to believe that she is not dying of cancer – until the last, she tells her that she's recovering. She even goes so far as to prevent visits from friends, so that they won't let anything slip or cause her mother to call a priest. Her retrospective justifications refer to signs that her mother had in any case suddenly abandoned her strong, lifelong religious faith. Beauvoir does not even consider the idea that there could also be secular reasons for wanting to know the truth in such a situation. Nor does it seem to occur to her that her mother might have the right to her own rituals of transcendence. If freedom only lies in overcoming the situation and moving forward, planning the path of a future self, then the last moments of life really are simply meaningless. If death is already in the room, one can no longer get ahead of it. Thus, while existentialism does not in any way deny mortality, it still has to suppress the actual process of dying. Because dying closes the horizon of freedom.

Staying as a curse?

After months of palliative care labeled as recovery treatment, Beauvoir's phenomenology of death sounds as if she herself believed what she told her mother: "it is as violent and unforeseen as an engine stopping in the middle of the sky."[6] And yet, for Beauvoir, this human engine trouble is essential. Not only for the kind of frail bodies that we are but also for our capacity to be free. If we cannot die, we really can't experience freedom. That, at least, is the claim demonstrated by Beauvoir through literary means in her early novel *All Men Are Mortal*. The protagonist of this exemplary piece of existential philosophy is called Fosca. And Fosca cannot die since he drank a magic potion in the fifteenth century in Renaissance Italy. Initially, this gives him additional powers and makes it possible for him to follow ambitious plans for the city-state where he is the prince. But, gradually, weariness and desperation take hold. He throws himself into adventure after adventure, tries to tie his fate to the Spanish house of Habsburg and its colonial conquests, lives through the Reformation, immerses himself in scientific discoveries, watches over the descendants of a particularly passionate marriage, and fights in revolutions. But what he develops in the course of all this is an ever-greater longing for death. His immortality alienates him from his surroundings. It spoils his friendships because he sees all people as already quasi-dead. It spoils love because Fosca's partners know that he is only capable of sharing his life with them for a fleeting moment. It spoils the historical battles because Fosca is not able to risk his life, and soon begins to see in every event the mere repetition of struggles that have previously failed. Immortality even spoils nature:

> I looked at the muddy river, at the flat savanna. At times it seemed as if the world belonged to me alone, as if none of its transitory visitors would ever contest its ownership with me. But then there were times when, seeing the love with which these ephemeral beings looked upon the world,

> I had the feeling that only for me was it deaf and mute and faceless. I was riveted to it and yet, at the same time, excluded from it.[7]

In immortality, from an existentialist perspective, there can be no freedom because there is nothing at stake in our decisions: things will always go on, there is no limit placed on time that would force us to take ultimate responsibility for the way we shape ourselves. If we cannot die, we will not only be bored – in the end, Fosca longs for nothing more than decades of sleep – but unfree, "riveted to it and yet [. . .] excluded." It might seem pointless to speculate on the potential freedom of an immortal human being. All humans are mortal. But it seems useful to me to clear up a natural objection to staying: that it has to turn sour after a while. I think Beauvoir misattributes the tedium to duration. The painful asymmetry separating Fosca from his surroundings could also be described as a power imbalance rather than an overly long life. The muddy river, the earth in general, might belong to him alone for a moment, and then they are once again faceless and voiceless. These two seemingly contradictory affects belong together. They describe precisely the way in which modern property relates its subject to its object: the subject is reliant on an object which it must control in order to experience its own freedom. It is riveted to the object. And yet it is excluded from it: the object must be lifeless and sharply delimited because if the line of separation were to dissolve, the subject could no longer claim to be quite different, sovereign in relation to its property. It would be a part, rather than an owner. Fosca's curse is that he is granted all the privileges of modern history and therefore succeeds too easily in being an owner. Over and over again, all his enterprises tip – rather like our capitalist world history – into acts of possession, taking control, appropriation. "One day," he says to the Habsburg Emperor Charles, "the universe will belong to you." "No one has ever possessed the universe," Charles replies. "Until now, the time hasn't been ripe," says Fosca.[8]

Beauvoir ties her temporal understanding of freedom, with its emphasis on pursuing projects, all too closely to a structure of consciousness which is not at all timeless: the self that must make other people into things in order to assert itself. If she understands transcendence as going beyond the self, she presents this in two ways: partly as an escape from a restrictive situation which – mediated by the realization that we are mortal – leads to freedom. That is the aspect of Beauvoir's theory of freedom which we absolutely must hold onto. But she also presents it as overcoming the external, so that we can experience our own will without limitations. That is the return of possessive individualism. Certainly, unlike in liberalism, the motif of overcoming is not static here; it is not about establishing a fixed external sphere of volition. It is dynamic, a mere transitional stage. Normally, death and other subjects who are our equals help us find our way out of the fantasy of omnipotence. Only then can transcendence succeed. But the linking of the search for freedom with the absolute claim to property is historically very specific, and this connection is elevated here to the questionable level of necessity, albeit as a transitional stage.

It is not only at the end of the novel that Fosca is defeated by his own inability to escape himself. His suffering – which is a mere shadow in comparison with that of his victims – consists in the fact that from the beginning he is fixated on appropriation. He confuses transcendence with usurpation. The fact that we are mortal is immutable, but it is not the crucial condition of our freedom. For if we want to cross the wasteland of mere staying, there is a means other than death.

Repeating birth

I discovered Beauvoir's *All Men are Mortal* through my brilliant friend and former colleague, Lea. Lea is unquestionably one of those people who know what it means to face death. But the absence of death in Fosca's life seemed unimportant to her. "Do you know what this guy's real problem is? That he can't be born again!" And in fact, it's not that Fosca inevitably loses interest in everything he does. Even when he has become completely cynical and tired of life, a new challenge or encounter can excite him again. He cannot find a partner who is not guaranteed to leave him. He cannot come up with a project that would put his own stamp on eternal time. But evidently, faced with particular people or opportunities, he can always begin again.

The notion that everything depends on being able to begin is the idea with which Hannah Arendt revolutionized existential philosophy. Rather than existence toward death, as Martin Heidegger understood it, she looks at human existence from the perspective of being born. For Arendt's notion of freedom, mortality is beside the point. What is crucial is that we can begin. "Because they are *initium*, newcomers and beginners by virtue of birth, men take initiative, are prompted into action," Arendt writes in *The Human Condition*.[9] She creates a new term for this quality of "being a beginning and being able to begin": natality, a term diametrically opposed to mortality. Natality forms the basic condition of human action in the world. We do not act as automatons or gods. We act as beginners. In Arendt's conception, freedom does not rely on our being blackmailed by the finitude of life: "its impulse springs from the beginning which came into the world when we were born and to which we respond by beginning something new on our own initiative."[10]

Freedom comes when we put ourselves in the right relation to birth. And the right relation is a repetition. In a sense, beginning means being born again. Freedom is self-rebirth. And this is achieved when an act is, in the first instance, something else, namely a beginning for the sake of the world. The existentialist idea of "self-making" is something that Arendt would see as a fantasy of control over birth, as a gravely consequential conflation of a new beginning with the production of something based on a fixed plan. After all, we can't choose our children. For Fosca's freedom, seen like this, the fact that he cannot give his life a particular shape through death is not such an insurmountable problem. He is born and could keep on matching this "born-ness" with spontaneous initiatives. Having so much time, he would even be in the best possible situation for this, if he weren't so fixated on repeating – in property – death rather than birth. Beauvoir describes life as the situation that Fosca is simply incapable of going beyond.[11] But life itself is not immanence, it is rather the basis of every transcendence. Duration does not condemn us to stagnation because we can repeat the beginning. And overabundance does not necessarily lead to weariness of life because we can structure it through new initiatives. Too much life: There is no such thing. On the contrary, if we are able to start something new with it, then we are free.

Beauvoir's emphasis on emancipation is essential whenever the situation in which we find ourselves is really a shell of solidified domination. Breaking out of that, however, can not only take place through Beauvoir's preempting of death but might just as well be conceptualized through Arendt's repetition of birth. Through this, the collective dimension of emancipation also comes more clearly into focus. We die alone, but with birth we come into the world and into the midst of people. "I [. . .] felt more alive than

I ever dreamed possible," writes the author and activist icon Barbara Smith, describing the sense of liberation when joining the Black civil rights movement and later the women's movement, and finally coming out.[12] For emancipation, our own mortality is less crucial than the fact that there are other mortals around. The new beginnings which Fosca does occasionally achieve demonstrate this. These are made possible by the fact that he seriously combines his interests and intentions with those of other people. He comes alive when he becomes responsive to others, rather than regarding them self-protectively as nothing but mayflies. For example, the fictional French encyclopedist Marianne brings about such a transformation: "Suddenly every minute seemed precious. [. . .] A hand was turning on the face of a clock; for the first time in centuries, I wanted to stop it."[13] The new beginning represents a break with monotonous, continuous time in more ways than one: first, it is a break with a time that is merely our own. The time of other people becomes key – it is Marianne whose projects make the minutes precious. And, second, it is a break with the flow of time: we wish it would stand still. Or perhaps it even does stand still, for a moment, so that the beginning is marked and counting can begin again.

Fulfilled time is marked by new beginnings, and multiplied. The repetition of birth starts a new initiative, its effect and its load-bearing capacity will be proven gradually, but its reality is already secured in the present moment, the moment of the new beginning. That also means that even in the face of death, freedom is possible. In the afterword to *A Very Easy Death*, Beauvoir makes a very dubious attempt to insist, purely hypothetically, that her mother didn't actually want to see a priest. But in this dishonesty, all those involved miss out on this real possibility. Maybe her mother really was just about to give up her faith. Not that this is very probable – but it's not impossible. When my French mother-in-law was at a funeral a while ago, an elderly nun suddenly whispered in her ear, standing next to her in the graveyard: "You don't believe in it either, do you, Madame H., all that talk about resurrection?" Simone de Beauvoir's mother, meanwhile, in the grip of both doctors and daughter, was not granted the freedom of such a spontaneous new beginning. Or of quite a different one. That she didn't have time was not an effect of her nearing end: it was an effect of blocked initiative.

Embryos in sarcophagi

Thinking about freedom from the point of view of birth means that even at the end of life something is left of it. It even means that the "store" of freedom is endless. Our time may be borrowed, liable to be claimed back at any time, but the freedom in it, and precisely the temporal freedom, is not. Perhaps it seems absurd in any case to conceive of freedom as a scarce commodity, but spatial conceptions of freedom tempt us to do precisely that, as soon as they give up the fantasy of occupying the entire universe. Stirring up resentment, they imply that increasing one person's freedom automatically means a loss of freedom for others – an idea with far-reaching consequences. Once, I even found myself sitting through a lecture by a speaker who insisted that the total amount of freedom in the world remained constant. I would perhaps not remember it at all, since it is almost two decades ago, but it just so happens that this talk was also my first date with Aurélie, who is now my wife. I was probably already rather inflexible with my daily routines, and I had said that of course we could meet on Tuesday afternoon, but on Tuesday afternoon I always went to the Moral Sciences Club, and maybe she'd like to come along? The Moral Sciences Club is a series of philosophical talks in Cambridge with an illustrious history going back more than a hundred years. The institution describes itself as follows: "If as Wittgenstein believed philosophy is a vice or disease of the mind, then Cambridge University Moral Sciences Club is a drug den or isolation ward where the degenerate or afflicted may fraternise in a tasteful or at least secluded environment."[14] This emphasis on decadent brotherliness sounds rather as if the chronicler was jealous of another hundred-year-old debating club in Cambridge which, despite a number of overlaps, was more a precursor of the Bloomsbury Group than analytic philosophy, namely the Apostles. The puritanical Wittgenstein left the latter group as soon as he was admitted, supposedly because the level of the discussion did not appeal to him. Admittedly, the "level of the discussion" at the Apostles included the rule that new members were expected to recline on the hearth rug during the first lecture. The club recruited male first-year students. Future candidates were called "embryos" who – without knowing what they were signing up to – were invited to "embryo parties." There, the older members took a closer look at them, and later voted on whether they should be admitted, in which case they took a vow of silence and their admission was sealed with the reading of an obscure curse. But back to the more philosophical Moral Sciences Club. Here, Wittgenstein himself was partly responsible for the madhouse atmosphere. The most common story is that in 1946 he threatened the philosopher of science Karl Popper with a poker, mid-discussion. To me, the much more bizarre anecdote is that in another meeting, the talk apparently continued uninterrupted in spite of a fire alarm. Be that as it may, when I was looking for the right room in St. John's College in Spring 2006, I didn't know anything about this background. I was simply interested in philosophy. I was staying in Cambridge through an exchange program, which meant that I didn't have to pay fees. However, I was only supposed to attend courses in German studies, not philosophy, a rule I ignored as much as possible. When Aurélie and I found ourselves walking for a second time along the same passageway in the enormous walled college, and once again crossing the Gothic "Bridge of Sighs," my new companion took the lead and found the conference room. I still haven't stopped getting lost.

The room was in the newer part of the college, and there was neither a hearth rug nor any hint of frivolity. The regular students who were there were probably either from very rich families or in massive debt. The guest speaker presented his theory of freedom. Apparently, there was a fixed sum of freedom in the world, derived from the scope for movement on the surface of the earth, and divided between all human beings. If someone was already standing somewhere, then no one else could occupy that same space, but all other space was open. The existence of power relations made this more complicated, the speaker said. I pricked up my ears: this could get interesting. But what was changed by domination was not the total volume of freedom, he went on, but its distribution. Slavery, for example, meant that slave owners gained increased freedom in proportion to the limitations they placed on the freedom of those whom they enslaved. No one came up with any objections to the assumption that there was always exactly the same amount of freedom in the world, regardless of whether or not there was an institution in it such as that of slavery. But a student with an upturned collar almost got the speaker into real trouble by coming up with a thought experiment that could have destroyed the whole theory: if someone accidentally shut themselves in a sarcophagus and lost the key, then the freedom of this person would be reduced without someone else's freedom increasing. Ergo, the total volume of freedom would decrease. People began clearing their throats and muttering appreciatively, furrowing their brows in anticipation. "No," said the speaker. "There is still the same amount of freedom. Because the man who is enclosed in the sarcophagus could do various things which he wouldn't have been able to do before. For example, he could scratch the inside of the coffin."

Aurélie has told this story many times, bewildered and amused, theatrically emphasizing her growing despair as she came to believe – until we left the event – that this precise occupation was my passion. However, that doesn't mean that she didn't get anything out of it. In its very absurdity, the spectacle had one great advantage in her eyes: at least it was unexpected. "Anything but boredom" is practically the motto of her life.

In Hegelian philosophy, with its complex notion of positive social freedom, there is a correspondence between freedom and love. They share a basic pattern, namely that of being with oneself in another.[15] We are free in relationships of symmetrical recognition, in which one experiences the affirmation which allows us to find ourselves again. That is, a transcendence which is also a return home. Well, I don't know what to think about that. Seeking surprises and constantly being surprised may sound symmetrical, but it still seems to me to result in a different picture. You are not with yourself in someone else. You simply enjoy being together, and somewhat beside yourself. If the freedom to stay contains an idea of love, then it is the idea that we share time without losing it. Or even more: that we share time and that through this it becomes all the more fulfilled, as the opportunities for new beginnings multiply. Staying – and savoring our time together.

This pattern of the freedom to stay is not limited to love. It can also transform political institutions and economic connections. Sharing time without losing it can actually mean not doing the same thing, and also not together, but relating to each other in such a way that no one's time is lost. That would roughly be the principle of a successful division of labor, in which all contributions count. Sharing time so that the possibilities for new beginnings multiply is also the principle of democratic decisions, in which agreement is sought for shared projects. The writer Teresa Bücker describes in her book on time (*Alle_Zeit*, "All Time") the various ways in which social inequality expresses itself as a lack of time. But where the scarcity of time is socially created, an abundance of time could be too, if we considered the fact that "time emerges between people and there is more time when we work together more closely."[16]

And, in turn, the enjoyable experience of staying mixes a trace of immediate happiness into freedom itself. In the work of Simone de Beauvoir, happiness is a category which genuinely runs counter to the all too warlike struggle to appropriate existence. In her memoirs, she keeps returning to its power:

> Happiness is a rarer vocation than people suppose. In my opinion Freud was quite right to link it with the satisfaction of infantile desires. Normally, unless it is crammed full to the point of imbecility, any child seethes with multitudinous appetites: what it can grasp in its hands is nothing compared to the rich harvest it can see and feel all around it.[17]

Here, the key to happiness is perceiving the world, and not appropriating it. For this existentialist, with her skepticism toward passivity, even such happiness comes from our own initiative: the child has a full, active desire for the world, at least as long as it is not numbed by false abundance. But what if false abundance is currently the rule?

This question is the theme of Kae Tempest's book, *On Connection*. Tempest is one of the most gifted poets and musicians of our time and also writes prose. A while ago, he came out as a trans man; the varied spectrum of trans identities, bravely lived out by individual people, is perhaps in itself a particularly fitting example of self-rebirth breaking through immanence. Rather than pressing two preset genders onto time, which always remains the same, people seriously and honestly accept the many shapes of their existence. And behind the language which seems to resist this shift stands a squad of missionaries of hate who should not have the last word. "Break those words open / Like a paramedic cracking ribs / To pump blood through a failing heart," Gabe Moses writes in the poem, "How to Make Love to a Trans Person."[18]

But back to Kae Tempest's essay, which discusses the fundamental human question of creativity. Tempest sees the source of creativity in connectedness – hence the title, *On Connection*. Inspiration, for Tempest, is a relationship, but this is systematically blocked by numbness and the deadening of the senses, so that the essay constantly wrestles with the question of how we can break out of our own limits.

> Life happens, but nothing has a deeper resonance. Except for the instinctive shock-back-to-feeling of childbirth or death, no action feels profound enough to root the person in an experience of life that feels purposeful. [. . .]
>
> I have been learning, my entire life, to place vast value on possessions, on social status, on public approval. I have to retrain myself if I am to learn to value the minute and gradual things. Small exchanges. Genuine intimacies.
>
> But how do I retrain myself?[19]

How do we get to the nuances, the reduction of numbness? Kae Tempest responds with blunt grandfatherly wisdom which I am happy to endorse – "Put your phone down. Listen to the birds"[20] – but also keeps finding powerful descriptions of the ways in which, in the middle of ordinary life, a frequency suddenly becomes audible which allows transcendence. "All that sound out there is life and people living. Not background sound. [. . .] Put yourself away. Let go of yourself. Tune into other people."[21] Other lives, other people, help with the transition from numbness to creativity. Something that initially only reaches us as a sound demands an echo and sparks a desire to overcome our lack of contact. That is not a seamless process; after all, something is at stake. For the power of our mutual connections, there is a wonderful formulation which appears at several points in the work of Judith Butler and resonates with Tempest's thoughts: "Let's face it. We are undone by each other."[22] "Undone" – the idea that we un-make each other, that we overwhelm each other. According to Butler, that happens constantly, in our grief after a loss, but also in every form of desire. We are undone by desire. We are undone by each other. And that is a good thing. It helps us realize that we aren't done yet, definitely not "done for," as Fosca thought he was. We need to be remade. Being undone is assistance in rebirth.

Rebirth requires heading toward the world. The shocking realization of another person brings time to a standstill. Afterward, our own time is no longer the same. If we adopt the perspective of connectedness, there is no such thing as time that isn't shared. The very self, the supposedly indivisible "in-dividual," is itself an inner multitude of voices and rhythms. We share our own lifetime with ourselves. Without the division of inner perception into tendencies of observation, of striving, and of discussion, tendencies which constantly communicate with each other, what Hannah Arendt called the "life of the mind" would not exist.[23] Without an inner division of time – even if it does not have to be divided quite so decidedly as Josette claims – we really would be numb. Time, divided into an inner dialogue, allows us to embrace the perspectives of others, as Hannah Arendt recommends in her theory of judgment. And in order to then be able to take action, we seek agreement with ourselves. "Self-agreement" is what the dramatist Kevin Rittberger calls this understanding of autonomy, in contrast to autonomy's standard definition as "self-legislation" or "self-rule."[24] Such a search for inner agreement requires time, like all democratic impulses. We must be able to pause in order to recognize what should be done so that we can continue living well with ourselves. Part of the desire that sparks new beginnings thus also applies to the freedom to stay with oneself.

But we wanted to come into the world, and not only find the world in ourselves. Using Beauvoir's imagery, we need to make the transition from what we can grasp in our hands to "the rich harvest" that we can see and feel. How can we tell whether we are succeeding – that is, whether time is being fulfilled? At least in my experience, in the actual moment of making a decision, we often do not feel particularly free. Time is running out, we have to act, and things might go wrong. Whether we really wanted what we desired is often not clear in advance. It is more the feeling after a new beginning that gives us a sense of whether it has been successful. The point is not whether the new beginning is due to a brave decision or to a lucky set of circumstances which we at least didn't mess up. Afterward, and that is crucial, we can find ourselves gliding, our existence suddenly light; it feels the way I imagine it would feel to have wings and to float on the rising thermals. In fact, the phases in life that really feel free are not the ones when I think every day about how best to budget my limited time, but when one moment smoothly joins the last. If freedom should be our vital element, we cannot reserve it for the heroic turning points. We must insist on its omnipresence in our ordinary everyday lives. I am not especially musical, but I can still remember when I was studying philosophy in idyllic Tübingen – having escaped studying medicine and found myself in a self-managed housing co-op – and I would leave the house, pass the hazel hedge and go down the steps into the old town, always with the feeling that there was music. A background melody which accompanied me and gave me the sense that I was fully alive. What made it free was the fact that I wouldn't have changed a thing. Fulfilled time: being totally occupied by what is going on but also not fearing that we're missing out on something else. If you like, we could say that this means appropriating our own time. But it feels more like surrendering to it. Because life presents itself in such a way that we can become completely absorbed in it, without drowning. The phenomenologist Edmund Husserl investigated the specific temporality which is necessary in order to take in melodies.[25] After all, there is always only one note at any one time, but you still have the previous one in mind and you anticipate the notes that might come next – that is the only way that the sounds can join together into a melody. A melodious moment in life might be similarly composed: the past continues to echo in it, and the present can be seen as a point of connection to the future. That would be transcendence, contained in a situation which we – for the time being – do not have to move beyond dramatically. We just have to go on living. Even when the melodious flow dies away, we retain the knowledge of this key. We can use it again. If that weren't the case, if we weren't able to hope for renewed natality, the harmonious gliding after good decisions and happy circumstances would be nothing but a lucky streak, which – depending on character – we could either enjoy or live through in nervous fear of what would happen when it ended. Being free means knowing that we can come into the world again. Not that it will always work. But it is clear that we can: we can start something with our lives. If that is possible, then freedom can be found in staying, too.

We are born unfree

In the Declaration of Human Rights of the United Nations, the universal right to freedom – the marvelous idea of Enlightenment philosophy – lives on in the slightly misleading formulation, "All human beings are born free and equal in dignity." Already in the French declaration of human rights in the first year of the Revolution, there was a similar statement: "Men are born and remain free and equal in rights." The idea that we are born free is a common theme in Enlightenment philosophy; it can be found in the work of John Locke[26] and Jean-Jacques Rousseau, who was horrified by the thought that humans were born free but were everywhere in chains.[27] As we know, this nativism of freedom came about in a world where some people were born unfree according to the law. *Partus sequitur ventrem* – "the one who is born follows the womb" – was the infamous legal passage which stipulated that every child of an enslaved Black woman was also unfree. And those are not the chains that Locke and Rousseau criticized most vehemently. We obviously have to take the best part of the Enlightenment formula – the idea that it really applied to "all" – much more seriously than it was ever meant. But what do we do with the idea of being born free? The achievement of the Atlantic revolutions consisted in confirming the freedom we are born into as our legal property. First, it is an entitlement, then an attested right. That would be the end of that.

But what if the opposite is true? Because that makes more sense to me: we are born unfree. We do not need a reference to inborn freedom to protest against domination. The extreme form of unfreedom that was established by the system of inherited chattel slavery obviously was not established by birth. It was forced onto some Black people for generations by slave owners and their societies. Meanwhile, the enslaved women, as Angela Davis wrote, "could play a pivotal role in nurturing the thrust toward freedom."[28] Freedom, even if it is passed on by parents, is neither in nature nor there from the start. What keeps people unfree, also after formal abolition, is the racism of others and its structural manifestation in batons and borders that don't target everyone in the same way. Angela Davis wrote the text quoted above from prison.

Someone who is born into favorable circumstances is still nowhere near being free from the beginning. From the beginning, all of us, really all of us, are exactly that: beginning. And from then on, we are here to set each other free, again and again. Sophie Lewis writes very aptly about love when she says that it consists in struggling for someone's autonomy "as well as for their immersion in care."[29] When it comes to the newborn, we can take this thought further: love consists in fighting for someone's autonomy *by* surrounding them with care. Loving attention is not an obstacle to freedom, it is its condition. We are really born unfree.

And we never stop needing to be set free. Being an adult means becoming more capable of freeing ourselves. One of the most fundamental forms of self-liberation consists in deciding for ourselves whose loving attention we seek – and what kind of attention. Not one single social contract but ever new agreements. We want to decide with whom we spend our time, and with whom we wish to collaborate in the realm of freedom. In its negative form – breaking off or limiting relationships – this can still partly be represented as the freedom to choose. But that is not quite right. We ourselves can be dependent on bad relationships; we can rely on forms of insult and abuse. For we are and remain reliant on each other. The unfreedom consists in the kind of relationship, not in the fact that we hold onto it. On the positive side, freedom is all the more reliant on being met halfway by luck. We have to find each other. And finding each other is only a precondition for a relationship. Or perhaps a relationship that's alive means instead that the finding never stops, that we realize again and again that we are being pushed a little more out of our state of unfreedom.

Overall, there could be much more freedom in the world. If time is bound in domination, we cannot draw an unlimited number of new beginnings from it. Phantom possession binds time. This is obviously the case when we are forced to be the phantom possession of others, but it also applies to the phantom possession that we hold. If you presume to make a claim on the lives of others, you cannot simply turn to the next project. You have to maintain the violence that ensures your domination. That, too, is unfreedom. Let's face it: we're all undone, and no one is done yet with the work of freedom. Where the real, historically defined time is pervaded with loss and violence, where the false, empty standstill of time prevails, we cannot step outside it as if we were stepping out of an individual situation. The situation reaches further; we encounter it again everywhere. It is not the individual life that has to change but the times themselves.

There are many forms of advocacy, assembly, and organizing that can make for political change. But if we look for the most powerful means to accomplish such change, we find the general strike. The general strike is a political form of strike. The 2023 fights against pension reform in France can be seen this way, as the strike did not aim to force individual employers to make concessions but the government itself. Participation by unions in the climate strike would be another example. Walter Benjamin describes the principle of the general strike by explaining that it is not about achieving better conditions for the same work, but about taking up "only an entirely transformed work."[30] Benjamin believes that the strike is not only a means to bring about a different time but is already the beginning of that time, "an upheaval that this kind of strike does not so much occasion as consummate."[31] The general strike Benjamin has in mind – the first so far in German history – was declared following the Kapp Putsch. A year and a half after the November Revolution, in March 1920, a group of *Freikorps* soldiers, hostile to the Republic and to democracy, had tried to bring about a coup by marching on Berlin. The government had to flee the capital temporarily, and in many cities there were battles in the streets. The putschists used the swastika for the first time, which had become an anti-Semitic, nationalist symbol shortly before that in internal conflicts over membership of the German Gymnastics Federation. On 13 March, the unions and Social Democrats called for a general strike, which was joined a day later by the Communist Party. A general strike means that everything really comes to a standstill – factories and government offices, public transport, newsrooms, and printing presses. In Berlin, there was temporarily no electricity or water. The leaders of the coup gave up after three days – they could not govern, there was no longer any power that they could take over because the power had been taken back by those who actually keep a society going. The general strike is probably the most complete illustration of how we can transcend a situation on a collective level. It practically imitates death – everything stands still, the life of a society is interrupted so that it can be reshaped in a completely new way. The idea of a political strike is still alive. It is echoed by the school strikes for the climate, it continues to be developed effectively in Latin American feminism, and it sparked the revolution in Iran.[32] The Woman*, Life, Freedom Collective describes the beginning of the revolution as follows:

> Jina Mahsa Amini was 22 years old when she was killed by the Iranian Moral Police on September 16, 2022. "Jina's death must bring time to a standstill. The cogs of society cannot be allowed to continue to turn until a different, new life is possible in Iran." This was what was going through the heads and hearts of those who gathered in Tehran at the hospital in which Jina died. Jina's body was brought to the Iranian city of Saqqez, back to her hometown in Kurdistan. Many locals were present at her funeral and accompanied her burial with the call "Jin Jîan Azadî": woman, life, freedom. Only a day later, people across Kurdistan used the weapon with which they are able to bring time to standstill, until another life becomes possible: a general strike.[33]

As a reaction to a fascist coup or to state femicide, a call for resistance was able to unite people. The shock of the event had already undone everyone, forced them to pause. But the call must be shared and repeated; it must travel from person to person. The more tenacious and long-lived the injustice is, the greater the numbness, the more persistently must the idea of the strike circulate in order to reach everyone. The Argentinian theorist Verónica Gago describes this process as a kind of underground communication by word of mouth. In waiting lines, in playgrounds, in shops, at union meetings and editorial conferences, the call can travel onward, finding its way everywhere, so that people can arrange a plan together, not only to opt out but to stop time together: "A *call* is necessary for the assembly. It is a call to *give ourselves time* – because it is in the assembly [that] [. . .] political time is produced."[34]

In a rushed, exhausted time, it seems paradoxical: the demand that we should take our time. But in materialist feminist theory as developed by Gago, a particular human capability is in focus: the ability to make time. We can share time without losing it, and therefore multiply it. And this is how the general strike imitates birth in order to create freedom. Gago says that the interruption of our habits should be lasting: not a temporary disturbance but a shift to a different temporality. This echoes Benjamin's statement that the general strike not only triggers the change that it aims to bring about but actually does achieve that change. The moment in which all those who live, work, and learn come together in the suspension of time creates an incredibly filled time. "Potencia" is what Gago calls this power: not superiority, but maximal potential.[35] The concentrated desire for a new beginning can be fulfilled in the general strike itself because everyone who would be needed in order to start afresh is present. They have brought their time together. No political time could be more fulfilled.

Usually, though, not everyone is there, not in this sense of a shared assembly for a new beginning. If we are lucky, we can at least work toward this assembly. But often we can't even do that. The expressionist poet Ernst Toller was imprisoned in the fortress in Stadelheim at the time of the Kapp Putsch, having been sentenced for his involvement in the Munich Council Republic. He spent March 1920 under extra severe conditions, in solitary confinement, without the smallest possibility of joining the anti-fascist assembly. In his letters and literary texts, Toller powerfully describes the experience of imprisonment, the horrific, empty standstill of time. One poem cycle from this period, however, is also about an unexpected visit which breaks through his despair. It is called *The Swallow Book*.[36]

I freeze.
The world congeals.
It must be beautiful to fall asleep
A crystal in the agelong floes of silence.
Comrade Death.
Comrade, Comrade . . .

Zirizi Zirizi Zirizi
Zirizi
Urrr

That one should hear such melodies
So drunk with earthly joy and melancholy
Upon the very threshold of the darkness . . .
Dream, my spirit,
And learn to dream the dream eternity.

Zirizi Zirizi Zirizi
Zirizi
Urrr

Away, away, Comrade Death, away, away,
Another time, later, much later.[37]

The call of the swallows becomes a turning point in which frozen, empty, motionless time is replaced with abundance, and the longing for death is replaced with the thrill of life. "Don't write that," says Aurélie. "It looks as if you're saying the same thing as the person with the sarcophagus: that freedom is equally possible everywhere. The difference is too small, no one will get it." I hope she's wrong. In fact,

Toller writes a few pages before that: "My fingers scratch the coffin of forsakenness." And there is really no trace of freedom there. He is inconsolable about the death of a friend and says that everything in the world is imprinted with the shape of his prison bars. He is not free just because he could do something different alone in his cell. But he gains a tiny bit of freedom because there is suddenly life that comes to him, with which he can share his time. That is still nothing like true freedom, and it only has an effect because swallows clearly mean something to him. But that is always the case – something has to mean something to us in order for us to be freed at all. At least the time of inconsolability stands still, as long as Toller's lyric subject puts his trust in the swallows' life cycle, helping to build their nest and eagerly looking on as they hatch their eggs. And then there is a scene – a scene which is also described by ornithologists – in which the swallows join together in a coordinated swarm attack and free a sparrow from the claws of a sparrowhawk. Toller celebrates the victory of community. And he does not merely mean community as an allegory. In the next passage, he calls for an uprising of the animals, of all creatures, against the domination of humans. That might not be an entirely feasible plan. But it's certainly a start. And it illustrates a dynamic of escalation in the freedom to stay. The company of swallows certainly does not reconcile Toller with his imprisonment. On the contrary, it awakens an insatiable desire that there should be more freedom. More and more, an abundance, for all the creatures, born unfree, whose task it remains to free each other.

3
Time of Abundance

A prism

What if freedom does not mean having space and is not measured by scope for movement? Can freedom be thought, felt, and demanded in terms of time? If so, the concept of the freedom to stay is not only a fleeting idea or an attractive paradox. The freedom to stay becomes a kind of prism, allowing us to see possible actions in the world in a new light.

In mathematical terms, a prism is created when a polygonal base acquires a spatial dimension of depth, as for instance when a square becomes a cube. With the freedom to stay, it is not the spatial but the temporal dimension that matters. The idea of "staying" extends freedom into time. This creates a new shape: the freedom to stay. Its contours, however, are anything but precise. They depend on how we understand time itself. A prism breaks the light in different ways, depending on its form. First of all, time is simply duration and – seen from the perspective of an individual life – it has a finite span. Correspondingly, the freedom to stay insists on the value of mortal, earthly life. Politically, this facet of freedom demands that the best possible conditions for life should be secured for all in a lasting way, and that this should happen now and not in a techno-fantastical future. From an existential perspective, the freedom to stay, with its acknowledgment of finitude, suggests that in the face of the unbearable immutability of death, we should above all work on staying – on ensuring that we see our friends for longer. Philosophically, the freedom to stay is an appeal not to flee from mortality – and thus from time. In this, it contrasts even with secular conceptions of freedom, such as liberal possessive individualism, when we look at them closely.

However, our imagination is able to bring any duration to a halt. It can expand what exists by countless possibilities. Through this, time comes into view quite differently: not as an unstoppable advance, not linear, but broken up in multiple ways by projects and beginnings. From the perspective of individuals, such breaks are starting points for a new time, results of individual initiative but also effects of our connectedness with others. Being free then means having time to begin, time for spontaneous new beginnings as well as for those that have long been desired. We only have this transcendent time if we are not tied into domination. Every emancipation uses the force of finitude by suspending something that exists. On a collective level, the greatest potentiation of such a liberatory power is the general strike. But new beginnings that interrupt time are also repetitions of birth: Liberation means coming into the world afresh. Every democratic decision can help us toward that. The new can mean self-transformation, but it can also mean expanding our relationships with the world. And, in turn, increasing our perception of the world means that we gain time: every new point of reference dissolves the boundaries of our lifespan by sparking a greater lust for liberation or a greater joy in staying. The freedom to stay, based on such a temporality of beginnings, is fulfilled time. We stay free in a time which we ourselves have decided to bring into play, and which we are able to experience as fulfilled.

But the multiplication of time in new beginnings has something too free-floating about it. After all, life is not an improvised concert. Our time may renew itself, but the world goes on ahead of it. Does the world have its own temporality? What would it look like, and what would it mean to find freedom in it? We would have to let our actions be free, not only by repeating death or birth, but by repeating the shape of the world itself. But perhaps the world is defined by the very fact that we cannot repeat it. And capturing the light of the world in the prism of the freedom to stay would mean having to start again with the conception of natality, the freedom to begin again. Because so far, there is a fundamental gap in the conception of natality: it omits the mother.

The order of the mother

The feminist philosopher Luisa Muraro – a legend in Italy who has not yet been widely discovered in other countries – writes as follows about the concept of self-rebirth: "The idea of bringing oneself into the world again, to the extent that it is in agreement with a culture that makes a metaphor of generation [. . .] makes us believe that we can make the work of our mother reversible or superfluous."[1]

This verdict also applies to Hannah Arendt's conception of natality and to my idea of a temporality fulfilled by self-rebirth.[2] Embryos don't just pop out of sarcophagi. We may come into the world unfinished and unfree, but we certainly don't arrive on our own. We are creative, but we are also creaturely, and we remain so: we are the work of those who gave birth to us. In her book *The Symbolic Order of the Mother*, which appeared in 1991 in Italian, Luisa Muraro takes maternal creativity as the starting point to outline a whole new relationship with the world and with the self. Or perhaps it's the other way round: she outlines a whole new relationship with the world and the self, and it is only through this that maternal power can become the starting point – the starting point for freedom.

Even in the passage cited above, Muraro does not say directly that it is wrong or misogynistic to talk of self-rebirth. She criticizes the image to the extent that it is conveyed in a particular way. And this kind of criticism already contains a large part of her philosophy. This "idea of bringing oneself into the world again" is not problematic in itself; it becomes problematic in the context of patriarchal culture. This culture encourages us to imagine a sovereign creativity of the individual rather than the real material basis of life: self-rebirth as an act of authorship, as a decisive battle with the self or as an achievement of construction. A patriarchal culture, according to Muraro, is not simply hierarchical. It is a culture that systematically robs certain bodies – mostly female ones – of their genuine creative power. The mother is reduced to "an opaque and formless nature, above whom the knowing, ruling, believing subject must rise in order to dominate her."[3] Anyone who has a potentially maternal body can then really only seek freedom in dissociation from that body.

Against this situation, which she also likes to call "symbolic disorder,"[4] Muraro proposes a concept in which the work of the mother is centered, rather than being reversed or made superfluous. The focus on motherly creativity brings about order, a point of reference that changes all relationships. It establishes a new symbolic order.

"Symbolic order" is how the theorists of Italian feminism describe the central interpretative patterns of a culture.

These patterns are reflected in language and determine its power to bring us together with our wishes and abilities. More important than the category of power, in this philosophy, is that of desire. In fact, the core idea is that equal rights and even resources and influence are useless if we do not have the means to articulate our desires. Freedom must be the freedom to desire authentically – otherwise there is no initiative, only aimless repetition. Such a polyphonic and potent freedom is not achieved purely through liberation; it requires a new basis altogether: a different symbolic order. That is the discovery made by Luisa Muraro and her friends and colleagues. They really describe it as a discovery, a shared finding. Muraro was organized in various different feminist groups, among them from the late 1970s the Milan Women's Bookstore Collective, and from 1983 the philosophers' association Diotima at the University of Verona. These groups recorded their process of political experience in a unique way, particularly in a series of texts, written collectively, with the beautiful title *Sottosopra* ("topsy-turvy"). It all began with consciousness-raising circles, which explored the political nature of shared problems and for the first time allowed them to grasp something like a feminine experiential horizon. But then it got boring, as the Milan group writes candidly.[5] Many of the stories told were oppressively uniform, and it seemed claustrophobic to identify with each other mainly via the common denominator of suffering, so they spent their time celebrating instead. Then they created places such as the bookstore and other meeting spaces, planned political actions, and organized international gatherings. These projects also kept reaching limits, which again sparked research in writing. And from this research, they concluded that their own weakness did not only lie in the strength of their opponent but also in the inability to bring together their own strengths in an effective way.

Or perhaps the strength of the rulers is precisely that: they can even restrict the desires of the oppressed, keeping them down. In a masculine symbolic order, feminine power has, in a sense, the wrong electric charge; it does not add up but neutralizes itself. No one has demonstrated this better in literary form than the international bestseller Elena Ferrante, whose female protagonists, especially the two friends in the Neapolitan novels, can never be happy and successful at the same time as each other.[6] In the political praxis of the Milan group, there were two antidotes to this dilemma: difference and connection. It should be possible to find ways of relating that involve "making the difference speak in free social forms."[7] And difference also explicitly means the differences between women. That makes it quite possible to connect this theory with current intersectional debates, despite the reluctance of some of its originators. The Italian approach is characterized by a furious fearlessness in the face of difference, which is not reserved for symmetrical relationships. The relations that help bring plural desire to light are mainly vertical. A test of whether we can dare to part with the patriarchal symbolic order consists in whether we are able to affirm female authority. And the proof that we are ready to face female authority consists in gratitude to the mother. But who is that?

Which mother and how many?

By "mother," Muraro always means both the person who brought us into the world and the person who taught us to speak. "We learn to speak from the mother, and this affirmation defines who the mother is and what language is."[8] That is perhaps not one single person, and it might not be a woman. What is crucial is that we did not do it ourselves. The figure of the mother forms the center of the symbolic order because, in her, things are combined which can easily fall apart. Both in the limitations placed on the oppressed, and in the alienation of the rulers, there is a gulf between reality and language, between our own experience and the possibility of communicating it to others, between our dependence and our freedom. If there were no such gulf, philosophers would soon be out of work. And Muraro's advice to philosophers is that instead of seeking ultimate justifications, they should make a new start, with the simple formula: "I neither brought myself into the world nor did I teach myself to speak."[9]

That's true. I, at least, can see myself reflected in this description – assuming I trust my mother's stories. According to her, we began to have extensive and lively conversations when I was about a year and a half. I can imagine it very well; I can practically see it in front of me. For some reason, when I imagine this babbling, mini version of myself, which I only know from a few pictures, I see myself sitting on a windowsill. That is very unlikely, but it's what I see in my mind. As if I had just flown in through the window, like the little bird in the German nursery rhyme ("A bird comes a-flying / Sits down on my foot / It has a note in its beak / A greeting from my mother.") Of course, this is once again a way of denying pregnancy. "The shared perspective of mother and creature," which according to Muraro we have to rediscover on a symbolic level, is a real phase of development in which we have already heard her voice, even if we can no longer remember it. After we are born, our mothers help us to make the transition into dialogue. "[B]efore we were able to speak with the other, there was a time in which we spoke only with the mother, and only to reestablish the originary common place."[10] This place, for Muraro, is the source not only of life and language, but also of our freedom. Because in every action, freedom comes from being able to bring life and language together creatively. Where the bird in the nursery rhyme is given the task of bringing a greeting and a kiss to the mother – "Because I can't go with you / Because I must stay here" – for Muraro, the work of symbolic mediation begins. Since we do not literally stay at the shared place, we must instead recreate it symbolically. Where there is a greeting, there is language, and therefore the material for that recreation.

Ensuring that we do not grow out of the knowledge of our dependence as children, regardless of how distant we are from it, is for Muraro the key to creativity. This means that the relationship with the mother is extended into an active negotiation. We respond to the fact that in one way or another, our mother's judgment brushes against every decision we make, because this judgment echoes in the language we learned from her. Or from our mothers, plural. Because for Muraro – in contrast with all those incantations of gratitude that serve above all to tie women to their role as mothers – what is crucial is that the mother is not irreplaceable. In fact, Muraro's definition is made to be expanded. "Mother" is a role that can always be transferred to someone new – it is the authority that gives us language and life. Because that transfer is possible, Muraro sees it as unimportant whether mothers in the everyday literal sense were "good mothers." The gift of birth is already immeasurably great; what more do we want? The Milan praxis of relationships consists in seeking "symbolic mothers" as orientation points for our own relation to the world – those could be other women around us, as well as models from literature and history. "To this relationship," the collective writes, "we have given the name *affidamento*, which we can translate as 'entrustment', encompassing both 'trust' and 'confiding in someone'."[11] However, like the mother herself, the mediating authorities that continue her work are not figures of identification. Freedom is maintained through the very fact that we can disagree with sources of authority without having to fear that those differences will be destructive.[12] That turns confiding in someone into the "free social form" in which plurality flourishes.

The symbolic mediation of freedom, which Muraro repeatedly describes as a circular movement, is therefore neither an anticipation of death nor a repetition of birth. It means naming a mother, making a connection, in a way that defines the source of our freedom in the limits of our independence. Separately from the quality of our relationships with our real mothers – and Muraro clearly indicates that these relationships can be terrible – our own freedom takes shape precisely at the moment in which we give the mother her symbolically central place. Rather than competing with the mother's creativity, we enter into a co-authoring relationship with her. In this way, incomplete attempts at self-rebirth become an inexhaustible continuing recreation. We are born unfree, but not alone. And our continuing births into freedom certainly aren't achieved alone either. From this perspective, the presumption of sovereignty – that is, the common notion of freedom for the possessive individual – becomes downright unrecognizable. It means nothing more than digging around in "dull, formless nature" and never finding the right beginning.

I do not know any other text that demonstrates the metamorphosis from domination and powerlessness to collaborative freedom with such striking clarity – and even with an underlying tone of joy. And after two and a half thousand years of philosophical patriarchy – think of how Xanthippe was thrown out – mother figures should not simply be ignored all over again.

And yet: of course that is a simplification. The symbolic order of the mother is itself not innocent of the metaphorical takeover of creative power. Just as a whole culture transfers language to us, our life is, in large parts, thanks to the work of others. Muraro accepts that maternal power can be routed through other figures, but choosing "the mother" as center and cornerstone of her system means that her picture is also limited. As a fount of authority, the mother is isolated, which draws attention away from the question of whether she was surrounded by staff or whether she herself spent her days looking after other people's children. On top of this, we are distracted from asking whether she became and remained a mother willingly, which is something we can hardly rely on in the patriarchy. In the iconic center of Muraro's symbolic order, trans men who give birth are ignored, as are godparents, fathers, and, well, the whole of the rest of the world. From our first breath, we also rely on resources outside the maternal body and capacity. There is even a hint of the same problem that Muraro identified in patriarchy in her own account: she might attribute some creative powers to the mother which genuinely reside in the social and in the biosphere. And that was exactly what this book was supposed to be about: positive ecological freedom, which comes, for example, with the presence of birds. Not just birds as suitable messengers from the mother, but birds as a source of their own surprises and offers of co-creativity. Does Muraro offer a transition to such a theory? This depends on the mediation.

Made from time

If we want to use common sense to capture phenomena that are far beyond our experience, we have to resort to images that remain insufficient. One of these phenomena is the age of the world. It is difficult for us to comprehend the fact that the earth had already existed for more than four billion years when our species, *homo sapiens*, emerged two hundred to three hundred thousand years ago. In order to make this easier to grasp, it is sometimes said that if the history of the earth were one year long, we would be the guests arriving at the New Year's Eve party at 23:31. Or if the history of the earth lasted one day: we arrive four seconds before midnight. Of course, this refers to the time up to now, but we often have the sense that we really are nearing the final countdown. Paradoxically, at precisely the moment when the Christian notion of the emergence of earth through a divine act of creation only six thousand years ago is fading, the sense of a coming apocalypse is growing stronger – an image of the end of the world itself rooted in salvation history. This is accompanied by a strange mixture of human self-diminishment and elevation. On the one hand, we are nothing, only a small entry in an unerring chronicle. On the other, we imagine that we are strong enough to put an end to everything. But what has been irrevocably destroyed by two centuries of fossil capitalism is actually "only" a brief period, even shorter than humankind's flying visit: the Holocene. That epoch, which has now been replaced by the Anthropocene (or Capitalocene, perhaps) began around twelve thousand years ago. It was in this epoch that a mild, interglacial climate system slowly balanced itself out, accommodating a spectacular wealth of species and a fascinating spectrum of ecosystems: from the everlasting glaciers of the polar icecaps to the tropical rainforests, from deserts to coral reefs – and, in between, a whole range of temperate zones where agriculture and human activity thrive. That is what we have unbalanced. Shortly before midnight, a few conquistadors and business bosses have smashed up the whole buffet. It is a catastrophe for most humans and most species currently living, many of which are far older – and perhaps also wiser – than we are. For the earth, this is only a variation; its timeline can continue uninterrupted.

Although our societies mainly tend to suppress any thought of the coming changes, it seems to me that exaggerating global warming and the extinction of species into an apocalypse is also dangerous. If we really assume that the world is ending, then the hope of being able to prevent this disaster – already a too grandiose and heroic hope – can all too easily become its opposite, at the moment of failure. Because where there is no future, conservation is irrational.[13] *Après moi, le déluge*. In fact, that is precisely the established pattern we need to break.

We have long been living in an apocalypse; we have simply transferred it to exploited people and colonized habitats. And we have long had an apocalyptic attitude. The theologist and cultural theorist Catherine Keller has suggested that we should see a connection between our using up of the world and the expectations of Christian groups, particularly evangelicals, who are waiting for the end-times. "[T]he religious habit of imagining the world out of existence would not seem to be irrelevant to the material habits of world-waste running our civilization," she writes in her study *Apocalypse Now and Then*: "in right-wing religious anti-environmentalism, for instance, the expectancy that Our Father will make us a shiny new world when this one breaks explicitly correlates with a willingness to dump this one."[14] In 1904, Max Weber made the influential proposition that the Protestant ethic that aimed at earning a place in the next life through privation in this one was crucial in shaping the capitalist work ethic.[15] It is perhaps only now becoming truly clear that this ethos has devastating consequences for the world – the world which is unnecessary for salvation and which is subjugated to work. The hard work of some is the apocalypse of the others. The Enlightenment break with ideas about the next life changed astonishingly little about the tendency to "imagine the world out of existence."[16]

Rather than finally seeking it in fruitful nature and temperate climates, secular politics put all its longing for the infinite into exclusively human history. When it comes to this history, belief in progress is beginning to crumble, but this still does not teach us how to respond to human finitude and ecological fragility. Thus, it remains tempting to merge them grandly into a spectacular event, an apocalypse, which promises the dubious comfort that at least everything will be destroyed all at once.[17]

If we were to locate finitude clearly in humanity, instead, we might be able to let the planet have its own timeline. But perhaps the timeline itself is a particularly insufficient image when it comes to capturing planetary phenomena. After all, it is, in turn, a model copied from salvation history – the span between the birth of Jesus and his return to earth. This understanding of time arose, then, when nothing was known about the age of the earth. The timeline, now secularized, had its boom in the nineteenth century, which was also an epoch of geological ignorance. In 1789, when human rights were declared in France, the Scot James Hutton developed the first concept of a more ancient series of epochs going back into the history of the earth, in an attempt to explain the layering of cliffs from processes of erosion. In his *Theory of the Earth*, he suggested that the planet had existed for much longer than had previously been assumed.[18] He proposed that there were cyclical processes of soil accretion and erosion, which might be able to continue for a practically unlimited time. Shortly afterward, this image was corrected by an English canal builder, William Smith, who proposed a structured development that could be divided into stages based on particular fossils. Without this massive extension of our temporal imagination, Darwin, a great admirer of Hutton, would never have been able to develop his hypotheses about evolution – there wouldn't have been enough time for the emergence of the various species to take place. But the reactionary backlash against Darwin also affected geology, with its claims that the earth was at least a few hundred million years old – claims which also contradicted the thermodynamics of the late nineteenth century. Only after atomic physics began to penetrate the phenomenon of radioactivity, at the beginning of the twentieth century, did it become possible to develop better methods of dating, which could determine the relationship of parent isotopes to daughter isotopes in rocks containing uranium. These measurements confirmed Hutton and Darwin's claims and helped us toward today's knowledge of the immense age of Planet Earth. From this point of view, within our own development, we only realized shortly before midnight that we were living in a world formed over a time span of 4.6 billion years. And there is no god who will help us build a new one. Perhaps it is not surprising that we have not yet developed an ethos that can in any way match up to this. We have barely even begun to grasp world-time, meaning that we cannot see what is at stake when individual species and ecosystems die. What we must understand is that this "apocalypse" was not predetermined, and nor does it come from the outside. We need to get a sense of how much in the world that could have been practically infinite has become – through us – liable to be revoked.

In her book *Timefulness*, US geologist Marcia Bjornerud describes our late-capitalist culture as "temporal illiteracy." In fact, she argues that we are "chronophobes" who hate time and live in a culture that doesn't really teach us anything other than how to spend less time on things. We are constantly desperate for technologies and advice to make things faster and more efficient, and we are surprised when the time we have supposedly gained immediately vanishes.[19] But, most of all, we don't have the faintest idea of where we are displacing this time to. And certainly not how much we are irretrievably using up. For Bjornerud, temporal illiteracy means that we are oblivious to temporal proportions. We miss the fact that "there is an immense asymmetry in the time it takes to consume, alter or destroy natural phenomena compared with the time required to replace, restore, or repair them."[20] In order to get a sense of these relationships, the uniform timeline of the age of the earth is useless. Temporal consciousness, or "timefulness," starts with the realization that everything has its time – that is, the time that went into its emergence. As a geologist whose research relies on putting layers of rock in remote corners of the earth under the microscope, Bjornerud emphasizes the present-ness of quite different times. They are there, present in mountain ranges which are not stationary, just far slower – and at the same time more powerful – in the flow of their movement than we're able to notice. According to Bjornerud, this means that in areas that do not contain many manmade elements, a different sense of time emerges, contrasting with that of the continuing arrow.

> Lost in my thoughts on the long walks back to camp each day, my mind washed clean by the sound of wind and waves, I have sometimes felt as if I stood at the center of a circle, equidistant from all stages of my life, past and future. The sensation spills over to the landscape and rocks; immersed in their stories, I see that events of the past are still present and feel they could even be replayed again one day in a beautiful revelation. This impression is a glimpse not of time*less*ness but time*ful*ness, an acute consciousness of how the world is made by – indeed, made of – time.[21]

As long as we regard the age of the world as an external attribute, it remains impossible to grasp. How many years was it again? Four and a half million or billion? Billion.

But what does that even mean? And stating its age since its origin suggests that it is still the same indestructible thing which has lasted for so long. Bjornerud's concept of timefulness suggests a different kind of perception: time as the essential core of the things it forms. That does not mean that everything is in the same flow of movement. The earth does not continually become more weathered; each mountain tells us a dramatic story of meteorites hitting, volcanoes erupting, and tectonic collisions. That the world is made from time means that everything has its own time, and in every object we meet a characteristic duration. Bjornerud does not make any attempt to decenter humans. However, the center is no longer a control center, but a minuscule point that opens itself up to perceive the spans and cycles that surround it. And that means perceiving the world.

Made from tides

Geology had its crucial breakthrough around a century ago, when it first learned to measure the age of the earth's crust. An equally massive scientific breakthrough is taking place right now, in the present, regarding the capacity of the earth to nourish life. It may sound surprising, but so far there have only been a few initial steps toward a "theory of soil."[22] We actually still don't really know why things grow. Yes, the magic of photosynthesis is understood by science. That is the crucial mechanism forming the world. Only plants can use the energy of sunlight to convert carbon dioxide into elaborate carbon compounds, i.e., sugars, releasing oxygen and producing the substances from which all other food chains begin. But plants need more than air and light for this. They absorb nutrients from the earth. Those nutrients haven't simply been lying around since the Big Bang – certainly not in a form that is digestible for plants. Moreover, the soil also holds water so that it is as constantly accessible for plants as possible. And the plants themselves, the soil holds them, too. Thus, soil has physical qualities – permeability and solidity – as well as chemical qualities, i.e., its nutrient composition. What is only gradually becoming clear is that these physical and chemical properties are effects of its biology. Soil is alive. It is alive not least because plants allow an enormous proportion of the photosynthesized sugars to continue flowing straight into the earth – the soil absorbs 11–40 percent of the sugars produced by plants.[23] Without the mediation of the life of the soil, on the other hand, plants themselves would not be capable of providing for themselves at all. The earth would remain foreign to them, and external.

The British writer and science journalist George Monbiot recently published an impressive critique and alternative conception of the world food system. His book begins with a cross-section of recent research into soil biology, which he approaches in very concrete terms: he digs up some earth from under an apple tree and begins examining it. "I break off a lump of soil, take out my 40x magnifying loupe, and find the focal length. As soon as I do so, the earth bursts into life."[24]

I must admit that as a farmer's daughter, I initially found it a bit off-putting to hear an excessively well-read *Guardian* journalist gushing over a spadeful of earth. What did he expect? Of course it smells and crumbles and crawls, of course everything depends on its consistency and on the balance of nutrients. Doesn't everyone know that? My own soil epiphany consisted of the reverse experience: the realization that soil isn't everywhere. Once, on a Greek island, I visited a volcanic crater. The earth was yellow and dusty, and we were told to wear proper shoes, not sandals. Obviously, that's the same thing I always say to visitors from the city before they go outside our house. But here, the reason to be careful was not puddles or thistles but the earth itself, which was so hot that it could burn our feet. A few areas of the flat surface were cordoned off and bubbled to themselves. If someone had asked me in a geography exam, I probably would have managed to explain that the core of the earth consists of molten lava, but at that moment I realized that I had never actually believed it. Some people believe that the earth was created six thousand years ago by a man with a white beard; some believe that we will soon get global warming under control using technology; I had evidently believed that the sphere we live on consisted of soil, through and through. That wherever there wasn't a rock in the way, we could dig and find more earth. Of course, I knew all too well that not all soil is equally fertile, and that it can be rich or poor. When I was four years old, drawing a portrait of my family, I drew stick figures of my parents and myself and a house (my sister had not arrived yet). I wanted my mother to show me how to write the names, and asked her to provide the following templates: MUM. DAD. EVA. SANDY SOIL. The land where my parents were tenants really was particularly poor. That was constantly a topic of conversation and led to various experiments with alternative methods of growing and selling our produce. I am really not imagining that everything grows by itself, especially not the plants that are edible for humans. You have to dig first. But here, visiting the volcano, there would have been no way to dig, here you would not reach the cool interior of the earth, crisscrossed by worms, but instead you'd find material from a totally different time, which would even burn your fingers. EVA, but NO SOIL AT ALL.

And, yet, all soil emerged from lava. Over millions of years. If there is already soil around, it happens more quickly, with humus particles being carried by the wind.

But "quickly" still means something between a few hundred and thousands of years. Soil is therefore not a renewable resource.[25] The fact that there is earth at all is anything but automatic. It is not simply a substrate, lying around: earth is the result of countless cycles of regenerative work.

Monbiot's description then quickly moves on to things that I know nothing at all about. The most spectacular finding of recent research in soil biology is the world-forming power of the countless beings that live in the soil. You probably already know something about what earthworms can achieve, digesting and excreting dead leaves and aerating the soil in the process. Well, the earthworm doesn't work alone. The order of magnitude – or perhaps it would be better to say the intricacy – of the life within the soil is overwhelming. In a handful of earth, you'll find more living beings – worms, insects, symphylans, mites, springtails, nematodes, microbes – than there are humans living on earth today.[26] And in one gram, a pinch of soil, there can be up to a thousand meters of mycelium, i.e., the threads that form the roots of fungi.[27] Soil is not simply made of weathered rock and withered bits of plants. It is less comparable with a pile of gravel than with a wasp's nest: like the latter, soil has an infinitely delicate architecture made from the excretions of animals. But while a wasp's nest is created by a single species, creating a bit of arable soil involves several thousand different species. About 90 percent of them have not yet been biologically classified.[28] Building the soil also means making it usable for plants. After various steps of decomposition, bacteria bring about this transfer. Woven into the threads of fungi, they are located near to roots, in the "rhizosphere," and react to the release of messenger chemicals by the plants. The rhizosphere is comparable with our gut flora.[29] We, too, are able to digest thanks to the activity of a host of microorganisms. But plants have their digestive systems outside their bodies in a shared location with the life of the soil.

The idea that "the world is made by – indeed, made of – time" is all the more true at the more effervescent, short-lived level of biological life. In organic life, it is evident that time has the shape suggested by Marcia Bjornerud's notion of timefulness: it moves in circles. Already in ancient philosophies of nature, the lives of plants and animals were understood as cyclical. I speak of "tides" in order to separate this form of time from spans and initial moments. Tides are cyclical processes of time, something that repeats itself as low and high tide and creates different states: waves in the sea or tidal shallows, for example. For organisms, there is a cycle from emergence till death, through which the species recreates itself in its individual instances. Already there, however, it is wrong to speak of undifferentiated return – then there would be no fluctuation of populations and no evolution. And even in shorter time spans, the circles are not identical; no leaf is the same as another. After all, no biological cycle takes place in isolation. At every level, not only when we look at the entire earth system, tides are connected into ensembles. There is a tide span from lava rock to soil. But the soil itself is in turn an ensemble of tides, a formation in which cycles with quite different radii interlock. The falling of leaves, rain, mushroom spores, and springtails and so on – they are all interacting in innumerable ways. The decomposition of one nourishes the growth of another. Precisely because there are nuances and changes, the temporal dimension offers a useful common denominator to relate the facets of life to each other. The duration in which something restores itself is relatively constant and characteristic for that type of being. Single-celled organisms, garden snails, and oak trees have different cycles. And we can also zoom in more closely on their regeneration. Not looking at the individual specimen, but reading its life in its metabolism: which nutrients does the snail need from day to day, and which does the oak need to live from year to year? The things that meet their needs are also tides, cycles of different substances. The tides only move in plural, even if all of them follow their own different rhythms. Life is a transformation of matter in tides – starting with star dust, from which ultimately everything is made, over time.

Dysbiosis

The model of cyclical tides seems to be in total opposition to the linear timeline. But it doesn't make the timeline obsolete. The movements of regeneration can, in a sense, be threaded onto the line. The long duration of the planet runs through all the gradually more diverse and richer loops of biological life. To us, it must seem like a straight line, even when from the perspective of the universe it is only a further cycle of the birth and burning out of a solar system. If we want to face the climate catastrophe, we have to take on the plural tides, rather than clinging to the fantasy that the planet itself could soon leave its timeline. It is the other way round. While the planet continues to exist, various tides leave it. And that sends shockwaves through other tides, which had been regenerating themselves through those lost tides. An ecosystem – a coral reef or a rhizosphere – is like a big cycle passing through other cycles that make it possible – as if all tides were ordered in such a way that the overarching cycle could be threaded through them. But the tides are not individual rings, one cycle after another; they are mutually threaded through each other in all sorts of ways. If one link in these chains can no longer close its cycle of regeneration, it does not just fall away itself but destabilizes other links. Because all tides are always also moments in the regeneration of other tides. A certain lack of stability is not a catastrophe – on the contrary, that is the stuff that evolution is made of. Without variation, there would also be no adaptation, and there would not be the constant growth in opulence which defines the Holocene and seems to follow Virginia Woolf's resolution: "I want to make life fuller and fuller."[30]

The familiar swallows, for example, come from a particularly young variation of tides. Only the human innovation of building barns and outbuildings, around eight thousand years ago, made their current way of life possible. Success in adapting – adjusting individual tides in order to be able to continue to regenerate under changed conditions – makes ecosystems more dynamic. However, if the pressure to conform becomes "unnaturally" great, due to contamination by toxic substances, for example, or rapid changes in the climate, this leads tides to drift apart from each other. Perhaps the swallows come back earlier, but when their brood hatches, the mosquitoes have not yet appeared because a dry spring has delayed their development. And, at certain points, ecological tides do not have any flexibility. Either a swallow chick gets its five hundred insects per hour, or it won't survive.[31] An individual chick obviously does not yet bring about a break in the tides at the level of the ecosystem. Even the gap created by the vanishing of an individual species can often be bridged. There are enough other points of connection for the tides that were linked with it.[32] Until these also give way. The biologists Paul and Anne Ehrlich used an analogy to explain this: It is as if we removed some rivets from a plane while it was in the air. One missing rivet might not matter, but eventually too many are missing, and the plane falls out of the sky.[33] Except that we can't simply build a new ecosystem in the way that we can build a new plane. And that point cannot be stressed enough. Ecosystem collapse is irreversible. The lost time is really lost. It is not a crisis from which renewal can emerge because the creativity – the circling time that shapes things – is shattered. If the collapsing soil becomes slag, we can see it as a greeting from the dim and distant past, but it will again take several geological epochs before something grows from it that we can eat.

In George Monbiot's description of soil degradation, he borrows a term from internal medicine. "Dysbiosis" is the breakdown of the gut flora, when the microbiological processes that should usually be arranged symbiotically get out of balance. This model transfers very well to soil – as mentioned above, in a certain way soil forms the external digestive organ of plants. It is here that plants digest the substances that thereby become digestible for animals, including humans. Dysbiosis leads to the collapse of system regeneration because the tides become disconnected from each other or cut off. Ultimately, the collapse reaches an irreversible tipping point – "as definitively as water flows out of a glass when you overturn it."[34] But dysbiosis only sets in slowly. It is easy to miss the point at which we could intervene in order to make regeneration workable again. For us, ecological processes often only start to look like crises when their outcome is no longer open.

When it comes to the soil, the decoupling of tides partly coincides with the very interventions that increased their short-term output of nutrition for humans. This is a well-known fact about the most recent petrochemical agricultural revolution: synthetic fertilizers wash out the soil, and immensely heavy, diesel-powered machines compress it. But recent research in soil ecology suggests that even the first technological improvement after humans began to establish a settled way of life and agriculture in the so-called Neolithic Revolution tended rather to disturb the soil than improve it. Since the Bronze Age, plowshares have been in use, and with the transition to the Iron Age, a good three thousand years ago, they proliferated. Drawn by oxen, they could dig ever deeper into the earth. Plows loosen the soil and uproot weeds. They bring deeper layers of earth, which contains few weeds, to the top. Plowing, especially when manure is added to the earth, turns earth from something that looks like a piece of hard bread into a chocolate cake. At least, that is how it seems to my human eyes, shaped by agriculture. From the point of view of the tides that make the earth into soil, things look different. In fact, they look downright apocalyptic. The elaborate soil structure is tilled to pieces; passageways collapse which could otherwise be inhabited by several generations of earthworms; the microbes that were gathered into rhizospheres are swirled into a mess; organic material is suddenly no longer at the top, where the decomposing organisms expect it to be; the layering of the soil, which corresponds to a complex division of labor, falls into disorder.[35] Disorder cannot always be avoided, and often it seems that what is regarded as order according to the demands of one tide is disorder for another. But disorder in the soil really also means disorder for all other tides. Where I used to think that digging was the work that made the soil alive, the opposite is true: it encourages dysbiosis. Real ecological peace evidently means that there should be neither swords nor plowshares. That is no small revolution in the symbolic order.

The slogan of this revolution is "no dig!" The relevance of this principle is astonishingly broad. Renovating old buildings rather than constructing new ones, stopping the construction of motorways and ending the extraction of fossil fuels – all these fit into the formula. No unambiguous direction for action follows from this. Not even the instruction to stop digging at all costs. Because from the point of view of human regeneration, the living soil alone is not enough – there also have to be enough edible plants growing in it. For this, the effect of reducing weeds has to be ensured in other ways, which certainly have their own problems. Weeding costs a lot of human time, mulching requires a lot of organic mass, herbicides mean contaminating the soil with poison, which has its own dysbiotic consequences. Further experiments are needed. Permaculture, agroforestry, perennial cultures? This example already shows us what economic democratization could mean: that the necessary deliberation would become possible in all realms of production.

If we want to keep the term "apocalypse" in play at all, we have to multiply it and reflect it back. Rather than waiting for everything to blow up, we have to learn not only to read the time of stones, but also that of the diverse ecosystems on our planet. Do they speak of dysbiosis? Can we recreate the shared place where the tides come together in such a way that they regenerate each other? And where we cannot do that, can we at least develop a better idea of our own influence? In the time since western colonization of the American continent, three hundred mammal species have become extinct; these species alone take 2.5 billion years of biological development with them. From today's state of genetic diversity – under favorable conditions, which we don't have – reestablishing this diversity would require almost double as much time.[36] Such cycles, too, envelop us.

In the face of this overarching destruction, the US biologist Robin Wall Kimmerer, who belongs to the Potawatomi Nation, writes as follows:

> All these generations after Columbus, some of the wisest of Native elders still puzzle over the people who came to our shores. They look at the toll on the land and say, "The problem with these new people is that they don't have both

> feet on the shore. One is still on the boat. They don't seem to know whether they're staying or not."[37]

Behaving as if we want to stay does not require preventing one big apocalypse. It is about small, nondescript, scattered, and yet omnipresent processes of dysbiosis, which we have to work against in order to prevent the collapse of the tides – a collapse that will only affect those who are most responsible for causing it when it is too late for all of us.

Unconstrained regeneration

Unlike humanity in its present colonial-capitalist organization, all the bacteria and mites and springtails could be said to be doing their work against dysbiosis already. But fundamentally, this formulation repeats the religious mistake of intelligent design at the level of worms. After all, it's not that they'd rather be having a rest but are instead working hard for us, or for the roots of trees. They are simply living. And in living, they are creating the basis of life for other beings. That is the miracle. Or in fact, that is the world. The world is an ensemble of tides, meaning a formation of regeneration spans that are interwoven. If humans intentionally recreate life – starting with their own – we talk of "social reproduction" or "reproductive work." This does not only mean reproduction in the sense of producing offspring, but every contribution to maintaining life, beginning with caring for small children, through every mealtime and every load of laundry, right up to psychotherapy and caring for dementia patients. In patriarchal capitalism, the majority of this work is split off from profitable commodity production, banished to private spaces, and delegated to women. Reproductive work then primarily means replenishing labor power. Even sleep, from that point of view, would be reproductive work. That is also noticeable in the quality of our sleep: "i do not sleep i press my jaw together with my eyes shut until a new day begins," writes the German comedian Ilona Hartmann, describing the attempt to get a night's sleep in late capitalism.[38] But there is also the sleep that does not feel like back-breaking work, sleep that we do not have to create, but which recreates us: sleep as a process of regeneration. Regeneration is the time in which something living is able to recreate itself effortlessly.

That sounds more like freedom than work. Whether an activity is work or regeneration is not governed by a fixed distinction. Marxism is based on the assumption that unalienated work can become part of free daily life: if work is meaningful and fulfilling, no one has to force us to do it. Whether work is also regenerative is, to a large extent, a question of time. It depends on the rhythm and the pressure under which we are working. I think about this every time I weed the garden. At a real farm that aims to cultivate plants efficiently on a larger scale, it would not be possible to work my way along bit by bit, looking at each tiny plant individually, and slowly detaching the roots from the rich soil. There would be no time. I would not inhale the scent of soil bacteria, which apparently strengthens the immune system and encourages the release of the prenatal and post-orgasmic hormone oxytocin.[39] I would be sitting on a tractor, or hurrying upright through the rows with a garden hoe. It is not only the capitalist pressure for efficiency that makes time scarce because it has to keep pay low. There is also the pressure of the tides. You cannot miss the moment to intervene when the seedlings are being suffocated by other plants. Then it is work, then you have to divide up your time because something has to be done and it can't be postponed. But if you are in the right rhythm and the planning turns out well and in any case survival is not at stake, gardening offers this incomparable happiness: you walk along the borders, initially without a deliberate plan, just paying attention. You can admire a dragonfly, or try out ideas for improvement. You pick a few things here, tie something back there, and pull out a clump of grass. Often, by lunchtime, you've managed to do more than on one of the hectic days. But it was not "work," it was regeneration.

In a world that is increasingly catastrophic, there will continue to be many activities in the future which we have to coordinate optimally, saving resources. In that, however, lies much less violence than in the alienated increases in efficiency defined by the market, which capitalism beats into us. When the forest is burning, not many people will have a spontaneous wish to go for a quiet walk. It seems to me that part of the suffering we undergo in the present is precisely that we constantly see the world burning on the screen in front of us, but we're not able to react in an adequate way.

The difference between freedom and compulsion often consists not simply in whether we want something ourselves or not. With many new things – and thus also in every educational experience – we don't know what awaits us beforehand. And it is also possible to be brutal toward ourselves, forcing ourselves into something we abstractly approve of. The difference between freedom and compulsion is often a question of time that is fixed and focused on acceleration, versus time that is open and unforced.

A large part of the natural world consists of processes of regeneration. But not everything is alive. Currently, the biomass on the planet weighs roughly the same as all the manmade substances (concrete buildings, metal and glass, plastic objects, textiles). At the beginning of the twentieth century, the manmade parts were only equal to 3 percent of the weight of the biomass.[40] Some of these manmade structures are essential for the reproduction of our life and no doubt conducive to our freedom. But all these things do not regenerate themselves, and nor are they worn away harmlessly. Most of what human hands make will remain on earth, and most of it is waste. An end of human labor is thus not likely to arrive soon, and part of our freedom depends on how we divide and organize this labor. But absolutely everything depends on how we embed it in the overarching tides, and therefore on the line where work becomes regeneration – how much regeneration we can rely on, which cycles we can keep intact or even enrich. In many places, it is still possible to improve the soil within a few years (and apparently it is not even necessary to dig it over). In the world of the Anthropocene, a world loaded with the results of human work shaped by capitalism, freedom is measured by the abundance of tides. Unconstrained time is time that does not cut us off from our regeneration. But our regeneration is, contrary to all the helpless advice about self-care, not an individual capacity. It is mediated through the world. We can only really regenerate ourselves in an abundance of intact tides. We need time. Because time is what we – like the rest of the world – are made of.

The source of our freedom lies outside ourselves. The paradigm shift that Muraro suggests in order to reconcile dependence with autonomy can also be drawn on in order to imagine an ecological freedom. After all, the conditions of our freedom, which lie outside ourselves, are essential. They are not limiting preconditions, not something we have to start by constructing or, if it is already there, cordoning off and protecting. We are not only free in nature, but with it. We just have to find a different beginning. The starting point for ecological freedom is not the sovereign individual but the creative relationship. For Muraro, it is the mother–daughter pair, a partnership which Muraro herself dissolves into a chain of predecessors and replacement authorities. That is an important lever against the patriarchy but not the only starting point. Every interweaving of tides can become the fount of world-building creativity. If Muraro emphasizes the importance of the inner attitude, the transition from denial to gratitude, what is revealed in this is a particular human ability. It is an ability to choose, but this includes choosing what has not been chosen.[41] We do not choose our own mothers. But we do choose whether we recognize them in the relationships that replace them. In the same way, the fact that we did not choose this planet does not indicate that freedom would mean escaping from it. Instead, freedom means finding nourishing relationships on this planet. We can replace regenerating relationships with repeatable tides or with scarcity and mountains of trash. We can act however we like within ecosystems. Otherwise, we wouldn't be in this terrible state. We are not caught in immanence or in an ecological niche; we can, as some traditions have for a long time, and parts of western science have begun to do, understand the interactions of various tides. In his early writings, Karl Marx formulated this as follows: "An animal forms objects only in accordance with the standard and the need of the species to which it belongs, whilst man knows how to produce in accordance with the standard of every species, and knows how to apply everywhere the inherent standard to the object. Man therefore also forms objects in accordance with the laws of beauty."[42]

The idea that we would be able to produce in accordance with the "standard," or proportions, of every species is obviously a hopeless exaggeration – as mentioned above, we do not even know most of the species that currently exist. But it is still true that we have this special ability to intervene in the tides that surround us in a way that is not fixed in advance. In order to learn their proportions, it is essential that we make use of careful, observational interactions, and traditional knowledge. Robin Wall Kimmerer keeps returning to the principles of the "Honorable Harvest" – honoring the gifts, never taking more than half, cultivating gratitude. These principles are based on a notion of reciprocal duty: they require that we always also give something back to the land, and they lead to a far-reaching promise: "Sustain the ones who sustain you and the earth will last forever."[43] However, it is not only the ecological integrity of the tides that is safeguarded through such an approach. The culture of gratitude also has another effect; it "plants the seed for abundance,"[44] meaning the confidence that we will not suffer scarcity.

Redundancy

We don't have to do anything alone. On the contrary, our ability to act relies precisely on our being connected with other creative cycles, from soil biology through midwifery to the division of labor across society. I know that bringing together ecology with Muraro's birth metaphors invites misunderstandings. "Mother Nature": No, nature is an ensemble of countless tides, not an individual, let alone an individual that tidies up after us. And she is more indifferent to us than most mothers. She didn't want us. "She" is not the right pronoun anyway; we shouldn't use the singular. "They," the tides, did not want us. It simply happened that way, over three hundred thousand years of evolution, that we go together quite well, at least we fit in better here than on Mars. "The nature of the mother": No, motherhood, including pregnancy, is in large parts work, not regeneration. But the fact that it is such an overwhelming kind of work – always with one foot in the collapse of the tides – is due to its patriarchal set up, not its content. The collective of tides demands that we call for the liberation of co-creators. Only if these can regenerate themselves without constraint will our freedom have a lasting basis. Forced tides fetter our own activities and end up breaking down sooner or later. Where the tides that accompany us break down, we have the choice between collapse and being overwhelmed. In order to avoid system breakdown, we can – as a creature with a certain understanding of the system – attempt to fulfill the demands of regeneration more and more ourselves. We can filter the water. We can constantly water the plants. We can fertilize fruit trees by hand. We can add nitrates to the leached soil and then realize that we also have to purify the surrounding water to prevent eutrophication. We can filter more water. Rather than using technology to increase our freedom and develop additional new abilities, in such spirals we then have to find technological crutches to achieve things which natural tides were able to achieve effortlessly. That is what it means to lose our freedom. In contrast with this, the more opulently that ecological life regenerates itself, the freer we are in our co-creative experiments. Ecological liberation means giving something alive its time. And in the same way, it is possible for us, especially when we know how to read the tides, to enjoy our own creaturely freedom. We can share our time with other living beings, without losing it. Sometimes this is literally what makes us. At the very least, it liberates us slightly more, toward rebirth. The freedom to stay grows with the abundance of tides. In a time of abundance, we have greater freedom. Not only because "more" is there, but because everything supports everything else.

Furthermore, the time of abundance is the best point of departure for the other two facets of the freedom to stay: freedom in finitude and in initiative. With the freedom to stay as the duration of staying alive, this is obvious. Life has a material basis, and this basis draws on ecological tides.

The freedom to stay refers to a materialism of tides. The very social differences that increase the mortality of certain groups often take the detour of "acts of nature." Rather than being assured safe passage, people are exposed to the Sahara or the waves of the Mediterranean. Work makes people ill, and, disgracefully enough, that often applies more to the worst paid work. Clean water, fresh air, and moderate temperatures are unequally distributed. Justice requires rigorous rationing of all scarce resources and an immediate granting of universal freedom of movement. But, then, all of our freedom stands and falls with the question of how well we integrate ourselves into the tides, how much they are able to continue to regenerate themselves, improving and increasing in richness.

However, the freedom to begin, self-rebirth, is equally interwoven with the abundance of tides. Because every beginning, as creative and unexpected as it might be, also means joining something that is already happening. It is like the moment in a concert when another instrument comes in: it affects the existing tides, on a planet in this solar system, in a history of evolution, in an ecosystem of the Holocene. The more catastrophic the world, the more closely our powers are tied to the most necessary things. The emptier the world, the fewer possibilities remain in it for us to bring in something new. Our perceptions of the world certainly have a subjective component. Even the most eternal world can be blankly ignored, as it is by Fosca in Beauvoir's novel. But where we open ourselves to experience, enter into relationships with the world, and seek moments of creativity shared with its tides, the possibilities are multiplied in proportion to the life all around us. More life really does mean more freedom.

A difficult point to grasp in Muraro's plea for a symbolic order of the mother consists in her belief that such an order is required for us to reach cognitive realism. The Cartesian doubt as to whether the outside world is only a simulation, like the fantasy of tech billionaires that they themselves could live on as a simulation, would be categorized by Muraro as an absence of a realist perception of the world. Meanwhile, she describes it as a great relief, thanks to the agreement between reality and representation in the figure of the mother, that we can stop "pretending" and reach a "true world": because only in such a world can new things happen.[45] Another description that she offers for this experience is "arriving at a way of being that speaks for itself [*si dice da sé*]."[46] I believe that something similar also applies to the transition to temporal awareness, or timefulness, as Bjornerud calls it. It would already be a huge achievement to gain clarity about our actions, to anchor them entirely to this planet, by beginning to negotiate our intentions and our plans for rebirth with the world. Mediated by the tides, we would come to see our actions in all their repercussions, and thus see them for the first time properly, in daylight. No dull *Weltschmerz* but enlightened reality. In addition, occasional horror in the face of irrevocable losses of biodiversity can be weighed against the relief, not to be underestimated, of finally being able to stop pretending that everything's normal: the slaughter, the insistence on growth, and the recklessness of letting everything collapse. Who really wants that? Who gains freedom from that and for how long, and what kind of pathetic freedom is it? Certainly not a freedom that makes it worth letting go of a much more comprehensive freedom, just so we can pretend that we're alone. Temporal freedom, then, means an abundance of time, and it means fulfilled time and abundance of tides. An abundance of fulfilled time in a time of abundance. If these statements seem to contain redundancies, that's a good thing because that is exactly the point: there should be no scarcity, and time should overflow. This overflow is the stuff of our freedom. It does not deliver us from the task of liberating each other in all tides. On the contrary: it delivers us *to* that task. So that we can stay – and not be alone in staying.

Coda

"Compost toilets should always have good views, but ours is exceptional," write Isabelle Fremeaux and Jay Jordan in their book about their experience in the "ZAD" (*Zone à Défendre*), an occupied piece of land in Notre-Dame-des-Landes, in France, where it was finally possible to prevent the construction of an airport after a 40-year struggle. Then they describe the view:

> With the deep green edge of the forest as a backdrop, the long flat field becomes the stage for a final aerial ballet show of swooping swirling barn swallows [. . .]. "It must be a sort of farewell ritual," says our self-taught ornithologist friend Alessandro. [. . .] Soon these swallows will depart for their six-week flight heading south to West Africa. For centuries, folk in Europe could not understand where the swallows disappeared to at winter; some thought they spent it on the moon, others thought they buried themselves underneath lakes or in the mud.[47]

Here, I have to interject: I looked into this, and it really seems to be true. That is, people did think this. The theory about the moon, for example, was proposed at the end of the seventeenth century by Charles Morton, a scholar in Oxford (I don't know what it is about Oxford), and continued to find support for a long time afterward.[48] But back to the swallows:

> Today, scientists have made detailed maps of their migration patterns, they resemble the maps in airports, colored

> trails crossing continents. But these fragile threads of swallow journeys, following the jet streams that form as land, water, and air meet, could not be more different, their flights don't flood the air with climate wrecking toxins. Many swallows die as they make the long crossing of the Mediterranean, but at least they can ignore the militarized borders and razor wire fences of Fortress Europe. Swallows still live in a world without states, borders, and papers, just as we humans did for most of our history, moving from one place to another in a slow rhythm of traveling and settling, leaving and arriving.[49]

The swallows represent just one of the countless tides that surround us and give cause for fascination and creative projects. Research into their flight paths, here, above the real earth, forms a little piece of temporal awareness, an end to pretending. And research into their migration cycles can give cause for longing. It doesn't really matter to me whether it's a longing to set off or a longing to stay. It just has to include a sense of time: an awareness of finitude, a readiness to begin, and a familiarity with the tides that carry us. "Every year, when the swallows leave us on their journey, the sky is suddenly quieter, less alive."[50] Do you know how it feels when the swallows come back?

Notes

Introduction: The Arrival of the Swallows

1 Thomas Hobbes, *Leviathan*. London: Dent, 1914, p. 110.
2 William Blackstone, *Commentaries on the Laws of England: Book I*. Oxford: Clarendon Press, 1768, p. 134.
3 "Danni" refers to the Dannenröder Forest, "Fechi" is the Fechenheimer Forest, and "Moni" is a nickname for the Seehausener Forest. Moni is short for Monokultur since the forest is a pine monoculture. Still, a monoculture is better than a car culture, according to the protesters, whose aim was to block a motorway from being built.
4 The German Nature and Biodiversity Conservation Union runs an initiative described as "Swallow-friendly House." People can apply or nominate others if there is proof of breeding pairs. See https://www.nabu.de/tiere-und-pflanzen/aktionen-und-projekte/schwalbenfreundliches-haus/index.html
5 Nina Simone, interview with Peter Rodis for the documentary *Nina: A Historical Perspective*, online at: https://www.youtube.com/watch?v=ySYRI4wXUpo

6 Theodor W. Adorno, *Minima Moralia: Reflections on a Damaged Life*. London/New York: Verso, 2005 [1951], p. 103.

7 Glenn Albrecht, "Solastalgia: A New Concept in Human Health and Identity," in *PAN* (*Philosophy, Activism, Nature*) 3 (2005): 41–55.

8 Michel de Montaigne, *The Complete Works of Montaigne: Essays, Travel Journal, Letters*, trans. Donald M. Frame. Stanford: Stanford University Press, 1948, p. 333.

Chapter 1 An Abundance of Time

1 Plato, *Phaedo*, trans. Harold North Fowler. London: Heinemann, 1971, p. 369.

2 Ibid., p. 209.

3 Ibid., p. 377.

4 Ibid., p. 279.

5 G. W. F. Hegel, *Phenomenology of the Spirit*, trans. Michael Inwood, p. 167. (G. W. F. Hegel, *Phänomenologie des Geistes. Werke 3*, Frankfurt am Main: Suhrkamp, 1970, p. 310.)

6 Plato, *Phaedo*, p. 401.

7 Isaiah Berlin, *Four Essays on Liberty*. Oxford: Oxford University Press, 1969, p. 133.

8 Axel Honneth, *Freedom's Right: The Social Foundations of Democratic Life*, trans. Joseph Ganahl. New York: Columbia University Press, 2014, p. 131ff.

9 Bernd Ulrich writes in a powerful and convincing essay in *Die Zeit*: "Since the Russian war at the latest, it has become very obvious that a society which is not prepared to do without some things and make sacrifices is powerless in today's world." See Bernd Ulrich (24.3.2022), "Sieben auf einen Streich," online at: https://www.zeit.de/2022/13/krisen-klima-corona-ukraine-krieg

10 Karl Marx, "On the Jewish Question," in *Marx & Engels Collected Works, Vol. 3*. London: Lawrence & Wishart, 2010, pp. 146–74, p. 163.
11 C. B. Macpherson, *The Political Theory of Possessive Individualism: Hobbes to Locke*. Don Mills/Oxford: Oxford University Press, 2011, p. 266.
12 Kathryn Schulz, *Lost & Found: A Memoir*. New York: Picador, 2022, p. 59.
13 The differing value of life, which makes some people ungrievable because their deaths are not seen publicly as a loss, is a central motif in the work of Judith Butler. Cf. Judith Butler, *Precarious Life: The Powers of Mourning and Violence*. London/New York: Verso, 2006, pp. 19–49.
14 William MacAskill, "The Case for Longtermism," *New York Times* (5.8.2022), online at: https://www.nytimes.com/2022/08/05/opinion/the-case-for-longtermism.html
15 Ibid.
16 Cf. Émile P. Torres, "Understanding 'Longtermism': Why This Suddenly So Influential Philosophy is So Toxic," *Salon* (20.8.2022), online at: https://www.salon.com/2022/08/20/understanding-longtermism-why-this-suddenly-influential-philosophy-is-so/
17 For a critique of the inferences leading to this prediction, see Janina Loh's informative book, *Trans- und Posthumanismus. Zur Einführung*. Hamburg: Junius, 2018, p. 106ff.
18 Nick Bostrom, *Superintelligence: Paths, Dangers, Strategies*. Oxford: Oxford University Press, 2017, p. 35.
19 Nick Bostrom, "The Future of Humanity," in Jan-Kyrre Berg Olsen, Evan Selinger, and Soren Riis (eds.), *New Waves in Philosophy of Technology*. New York: Palgrave Macmillan, 2009, pp. 186–215, p. 204.

20 Raffi Khatchadourian, "The Doomsday Invention," *New Yorker* (23.11.2015), online at: https://www.newyorker.com/magazine/2015/11/23/doomsday-invention-artificial-intelligence-nick-bostrom

21 Cf. Nick Bostrom, "Astronomical Waste: The Opportunity Cost of Delayed Technological Development," *Utilitas* 15(3) (2003): 308–14.

22 For a more detailed reconstruction of Arendt's alternative theory of possessive individualism, see Eva von Redecker, "Authoritarian Accumulation: Hannah Arendt on Hobbes' Leviathan and Bourgeois History," in Guido Frilli (ed.), *Hobbes nel Novecento*. Naples: Istituto Italiano per gli Studi Filosofici Press, 2022, pp. 157–74.

23 Hannah Arendt, *The Origins of Totalitarianism*. San Diego/New York/London: Harcourt Brace, 1973, p. 142.

24 Ibid., p. 144.

25 Nicholas Beckstead, *On the Overwhelming Importance of Shaping the Far Future*. Dissertation for the degree of Doctor of Philosophy. Brunswick: The State University of New Jersey 2013, p. 11, online at: https://rucore.libraries.rutgers.edu/rutgers-lib/40469/PDF/1/play/

26 Octavia E. Butler, *Parable of the Sower*. London: Headline, 2014, p. 84.

Chapter 2 Fulfilled Time

1 Virginia Woolf, *The Diary of Virginia Woolf: Volume 2: 1920–1924*, ed. Anne Olivier Bell. Orlando, FL: Harcourt Brace, 1987, p. 237.

2 Pierre Charbonnier, *Affluence and Freedom: An Environmental History of Political Ideas*, trans. Andrew Brown. Cambridge, UK/Medford, MA: Polity Press, 2021, pp. 10–11.

3 Cf. Hannah Arendt, *The Life of the Mind*. San Diego/New York/London: Harcourt, 1978, p. 191. A detailed

reconstruction of Hannah Arendt's theory of judgment can be found here: Eva von Redecker, *Gravitation zum Guten. Hannah Arendts Moralphilosophie*. Berlin: Lukas Verlag, 2013.

4 Simone de Beauvoir, *The Second Sex*, trans. Constance Borde and Sheila Malovany-Chevallier. New York: Knopf, 2010, p. 17.

5 Simone de Beauvoir, *A Very Easy Death*, trans. Patrick O'Brian. New York: Pantheon 1985, p. 57.

6 Ibid., p. 106.

7 Simone de Beauvoir, *All Men Are Mortal*, trans. Leonard M. Friedman. New York/London: Norton, 1992, p. 222.

8 Ibid., p. 156.

9 Hannah Arendt, *The Human Condition*. Chicago/London: University of Chicago Press, 1998, p. 177.

10 Ibid.

11 In contrast with this, Karen Ng has shown that in the original Hegelian dialectics, life is the only category whose immediacy need not be sublated in the course of self-realization. Cf. Karen Ng, *Hegel's Concept of Love: Self-Consciousness, Freedom, Logic*. Oxford: Oxford University Press, 2020.

12 Cited according to Robin D. Kelley, *Freedom Dreams: The Black Radical Imagination*. Boston: Beacon Press, 2002, p. 136.

13 Beauvoir, *All Men Are Mortal*, p. 267.

14 Hugh Mellor, "The Moral Sciences Club (A Short History)," online at: https://www.phil.cam.ac.uk/seminars-phil/seminars-msc-history

15 G. W. F. Hegel, *Elements of the Philosophy of Right*, ed. Allen W. Wood, trans. H. B. Nesbit. Cambridge: Cambridge University Press, 1991, p. 42.

16 Teresa Bücker, *Alle_Zeit. Eine Frage von Macht und Freiheit*. Berlin: Ullstein, 2022, p. 15. Quotation trans. by LD.

17 Simone de Beauvoir, *The Prime of Life: The Autobiography of Simone de Beauvoir*, trans. Peter Green. New York: Paragon House 1992, p. 27.
18 Cited according to Jules Joanne Gleeson, "How Do Gender Transitions Happen?," in Jules Joanne Gleeson and Elle O'Rourke (eds.), *Transgender Marxism*. London: Pluto Press, 2021, p. 80.
19 Kae Tempest, *On Connection*. London: Faber, 2020, pp. 112–14.
20 Ibid., p. 115.
21 Ibid., p. 117.
22 See, e.g., Judith Butler, *Undoing Gender*. New York and Abingdon: Routledge, 2004, p. 19.
23 Arendt, *The Life of the Mind*.
24 Kevin Rittberger, "Autonomie," in *Autonomie. Spielzeit 2021/2022*. Hanover: Schauspiel, Hannover, 2021. Quotation trans. by LD.
25 Edmund Husserl, *The Phenomenology of Internal Time-Consciousness*, trans. James S. Churchill. Bloomington, IN: Indiana University Press, 2019, p. 30.
26 Locke is very much aware of children's dependence and writes that "man is born with [. . .] a right of freedom to his person." John Locke, *Second Treatise of Government*. New York: Liberal Arts Press 1952, p. 107.
27 Jean-Jacques Rousseau, *The Social Contract*, trans. Maurice Cranston. London: Penguin 1968, p. 49.
28 Angela Davis, "Reflections on the Black Woman's Role in the Community of Slaves," *Massachusetts Review* 13(1/2) (1972): 81–100, 96.
29 Sophie Lewis, *Abolish the Family*. London/New York: Verso, 2022, p. 2.
30 Walter Benjamin, *Toward the Critique of Violence: A Critical Edition*, trans. and ed. Peter Fenves and Julia Ng. Redwood City, CA: Stanford University Press, 2021, p. 52.

31 Ibid.
32 For a more detailed discussion of current forms of protest, including Fridays for Future and feminist strikes, see Eva von Redecker, *Revolution für das Leben. Philosophie der neuen Protestformen*. Frankfurt am Main: Fischer, 2020.
33 Woman*, Life, Freedom Kollektiv (2022), "Streiken bis zum Umsturz. Die Rolle der Streikenden in der gegenwärtigen Revolution im Iran," online at: https://www.rosalux.de/news/id/49747/streiken-bis-zum-umsturz/ Quotation trans. by LD.
34 Verónica Gago, *Feminist International: How to Change Everything*, trans. Liz Mason-Deese. London/New York: Verso, 2020, p. 163.
35 Ibid., p. 2.
36 Toller also mentions the swallows' visit in his letters. Cf. Ernst Toller, "An Netti Katzenstein, 22. Mai 1921," in Stefan Neuhaus et al. (eds.), *Ernst Toller: Briefe 1915–1939*. Göttingen: Wallstein Verlag 2018, p. 165; and Ernst Toller, "An Netti Katzenstein, 23. Juni 1922," ibid., p. 271.
37 Ernst Toller, *The Swallow Book*, trans. Ashley Dukes. Oxford: Oxford University Press, 1924, pp. 8–9.

Chapter 3 Time of Abundance

1 Luisa Muraro, *The Symbolic Order of the Mother*, trans. Francesca Novello, ed. Timothy S. Murphy. New York: SUNY Press, 2018, p. 19.
2 The fact that Hannah Arendt's conception of natality leaves out parenting and pregnancy is also emphasized by Luisa Muraro's colleague, Adriana Cavarero; cf. Adriana Cavarero, *Inclinations: A Critique of Rectitude*, trans. Amanda Minervini and Adam Sitze. Stanford, CA: Stanford University Press, 2016, pp. 102, 104.

3 Muraro, *The Symbolic Order of the Mother*, p. 7.
4 Ibid., p. 58.
5 The Milan Women's Bookstore Collective, *Sexual Difference: A Theory of Social-Symbolic Practice*, trans. Patricia Cicogna and Teresa de Lauretis. Bloomington, IN: Indiana University Press, 1990, p. 45.
6 In interviews, Ferrante has repeatedly referred to Luisa Muraro's strong influence on her thinking; cf. Elena Ferrante, *Frantumaglia: A Writer's Journey*, trans. Ann Goldstein. New York: Europa Editions, 2016, p. 332.
7 Milan Women's Bookstore Collective, *Sexual Difference*, p. 132.
8 Muraro, *The Symbolic Order of the Mother*, p. 43.
9 Ibid., p. 96.
10 Ibid., p. 63.
11 Libreria delle donne di Milano (Laura Balestrini, Maria Grazia Campari, Traudel Sattler), "... Nicht glauben, Rechte zu haben," in Astrid Deuber-Mankowsky, Ulrike Ramming, and E. Walesca Tielsch (eds.), *1789/1989. Die Revolution hat nicht stattgefunden.* Tübingen: Edition Diskord, 1989, pp. 253–60, p. 256. Quotation amended and trans. by LD.
12 On this point, cf. Diana Sartori, "'Du sollst.' Ein mütterliches Gebot," in *Diotima: Jenseits der Gleichheit. Über Macht und die weiblichen Wurzeln der Autorität.* Königstein: Ulrike Helmer Verlag, 1999, pp. 11–44, p. 27.
13 Cf. Marcia Bjornerud, *Timefulness: How Thinking Like a Geologist Can Help Save the World.* Princeton/Oxford: Princeton University Press, 2020, p. 11.
14 Catherine Keller, *Apocalypse Now and Then: A Feminist Guide to the End of the World.* Boston: Beacon Press, 1996, p. 2.

15 Max Weber, *The Protestant Ethic and the "Spirit" of Capitalism and Other Writings*, trans. and ed. Peter Baehr and Gordon C. Wells. New York: Penguin, 2002.
16 Cf. also Hannah Arendt, *Fragwürdige Traditionsbestände im politischen Denken der Gegenwart*, trans. Charlotte Beradt. Munich: Piper, 2021, p. 114f.
17 Keller, *Apocalypse Now and Then*, p. 85.
18 This account follows Marcia Bjornerud, *Timefulness*, p. 23ff.
19 For a powerful description of this phenomenon, see also Hartmut Rosa, *Social Acceleration: A New Theory of Modernity*, trans. Jonathan Trejo-Mathys. New York: Columbia, p. 131ff.
20 Cf. Bjornerud, *Timefulness*, p. 157.
21 Ibid., p. 5.
22 Cf. George Monbiot, *Regenesis: Feeding the World without Devouring the Planet*. London: Penguin, 2022, p. 23.
23 Ibid., p. 15.
24 Ibid., p. 9.
25 Frauke Fischer and Hilke Oberhansberg, *Was hat die Mücke je für uns getan? Endlich verstehen, was biologische Vielfalt für unser Leben bedeutet*. Munich: Oekom, 2020, p. 63.
26 Ibid.
27 Monbiot, *Regenesis*, p. 14.
28 Ibid., p. 8.
29 Ibid., p. 17.
30 Woolf, *The Diary of Virginia Woolf*, 1987, p. 237. See also p. 57 in this book.
31 Stephen Moss, *The Swallow: A Biography*. London: Square Peg, 2020, p. 72.
32 In the case of the Permian Triassic mass extinction, that has now been shown, cf. Damian Carrington, "Ecosystem

Collapse 'Inevitable' unless Wildlife Losses Reversed," *Guardian* (24.2.2023), online at: https://www.theguardian.com/environment/2023/feb/24/ecosystem-collapse-wildlife-losses-permian-triassic-mass-extinction-study

33 Paul and Anne Ehrlich, *Extinction: The Causes and Consequences of the Disappearance of Species*. London: Gollancz, 1982, p. xi ff. See also Josef Settele's explanation in Fritz Reheis, *Erhalten und Erneuern. Nur Kreisläufe sind nachhaltig, Durchläufe nicht*. Hamburg: VSA, 2022, p. 45.

34 Schulz, *Lost & Found*, p. 59.

35 Cf. Monbiot, *Regenesis*, p. 155.

36 Fischer and Oberhansberg, *Was hat die Mücke je für uns getan?*, p. 29.

37 Robin Wall Kimmerer, *Braiding Sweetgrass: Indigenous Wisdom, Scientific Knowledge and the Teachings of Plants*. London: Penguin, 2020, p. 207.

38 Ilona Hartman (@zirkuspony) on Instagram (26.2.2023). Quotation translated by LD.

39 Kimmerer, *Braiding Sweetgrass*, p. 236.

40 Maddie Stone, "Human-made materials now equal weight of all life on Earth," *National Geographic* (9.12.2020), online at: https://www.nationalgeographic.com/environment/article/human-made-materials-now-equal-weight-of-all-life-on-earth

41 Cf. Sabine Hark, *Gemeinschaft der Ungewählten: Umrisse eines politischen Ethos der Kohabitation*. Berlin: Suhrkamp, 2021.

42 Marx, "Economic and Philosophic Manuscripts of 1844," in *Marx & Engels Collected Works, Vol. 3*, pp. 229–346, p. 277.

43 Kimmerer, *Braiding Sweetgrass*, p. 183.

44 Ibid., p. 376.

45 Muraro, *The Symbolic Order of the Mother*, pp. 29, 75.

46 Ibid., p. 30.

47 Isabelle Fremeaux and Jay Jordan, *We Are "Nature" Defending Itself: Entangling Art, Activism, and Autonomous Zones*. London: Pluto Press, 2021, pp. 24–7.
48 Moss, *The Swallow*, p. 136.
49 Fremeaux and Jordan, *We Are "Nature" Defending Itself*, pp. 27–8.
50 Ibid., p. 28.

Acknowledgments

I am grateful to Yelenah Frahm for her unique calm and for her enthusiasm, and for the way each sentence gets so much better in her hands.

I am grateful to Barbara Wenner for her indispensable support, for so much time, for trust and confidence, and for her excellent sense of proportion.

I would like to thank Fulvia Modica for several years of collaboration: the stars were aligned when we began working together.

I have had many conversations about the freedom to stay, and I am indebted to all those who talked to me, particularly Elisabeth Bonsen, Ann Copestake, Pascale Evrard, Raymond Geuss, Jan Groos, Amira Möding, Lea-Riccarda Prix, Susanne von Redecker, Matěj Spurný, Oskar Spurný, and Elisabeth von Thadden.

Several people looked at individual chapters and helped me immeasurably with their criticisms and suggestions: Birte de Gruisborne, Marx Harder, Fulvia Modica, Amira Möding, Samia Mohammed, Abibi Stewart, and the Lübeck group of female philosophers.

I am grateful to Sophie von Redecker, Solvejg Harder and Helen Barr for putting their trust in me.

I would also like to thank the FrAK (Frankfurter Arbeitskreis für politische Theorie) for so many years of fruitful discussions, the Wildcat Colloquium for a great year of background reading, and the SALT collective for promising beginnings, TANNA for kindly inviting me into Italian feminism (and other feminisms), and the editors of the *Wandelblatt* for their political work in our region.

Aurélie and Lucy provide me with the most creative freedom to stay that I can imagine – aka the Six O'Clock Society; Ann is always there for me, and Evelyn, Heike, Matthias/Jennifer, Maggie, Nina, Mona, Sophie, and Stefan give me so much more than a home.

March 2023

Lucy Duggan began translating this work before we knew it was going to be published. I'm immensely lucky to have her friendship and translation; she's a genius at both.

I'm very grateful to John Thompson at Polity for his enthusiasm for the book and for the swallows.

Many colleagues and friends have probed ideas from this book with me since it first appeared. I want to thank in particular Ingrid Leijten, Andreas Folkers, Wolfgang Kaleck, Juliane Rebentisch and Eva Horn. My deepest debt is to Wendy Brown, who keeps convincing me that this work isn't done yet.